Chöd in the Ganden Tradition

Chöd in the Ganden Tradition

The Oral Instructions of Kyabje Zong Rinpoche

by Kyabje Zong Rinpoche

edited by David Molk

SNOW LION PUBLICATIONS

ITHACA, NEW YORK • BOULDER, COLORADO

Snow Lion Publications
P.O. Box 6483
Ithaca, New York 14851 USA
607-273-2542
www.snowlionpub.com

Printed in Canada on acid-free, recycled paper.
Designed and typeset by Gopa & Ted2, Inc.

ISBN-13: 978-1-55939-261-7
ISBN-10: 1-55939-261-4

Library of Congress Cataloging-in-Publication Data

ᵔ⌒Table of Contents

Kyabje Zong Rinpoche: A Biographical Profile   13

Introduction: The "Sacred Cutting" of Chöd   27
   Taking Vast Scriptural Learning as Personal Advice   28
   Kyabje Zong Rinpoche and His Previous Lives   29
   Transcending Partisanship   38
   Dialectical Debate and the Middle Way   41
   Putting Study to Use in Practice   45
   Maintaining Pure View of the Guru   48
   Practicing with the Wisdom of Compassion   50

CHÖD IN THE GANDEN TRADITION: THE ORAL INSTRUCTIONS

An Overview of the Practice of Chöd   55
   Lineage of the Practice   55
   Place of Practice   59
   Basis for Practice   62
   Advice on Practice   67

Preliminary Practices of Chöd
   Going for Refuge and Generating Bodhichitta   71
   Guru Yoga: Gateway to Empowering Blessings   74
   Accumulating Merit through Seven-limb Prayer and Mandala Offering   77

Purifying Obstructions and Nonvirtue through
  the Descent of Nectar from AH   85

Actual Practice of Chöd: Gathering the Two Accumulations   95

  Gathering the Accumulation of Merit
  by Offering the Illusory Body   95
    The White Distribution   95
    The Red Distribution   104
    The Manifold Distribution   108
    Giving Dharma and Meditating on Taking and Giving   111

  Gathering the Accumulation of Wisdom
  through Meditation on Emptiness   119
    The Three Spheres of Giving   120
    The Logical Reasons   123
    Three Methods for Meditation on Emptiness in Chöd Practice   131

  Mara Hindrances in Chöd Practice   133

  Dedicating the Accumulations to Unsurpassed
  Great Enlightenment   138

Concluding Advice   141

  Use of the Ritual Damaru and Thighbone Trumpet   141

  The Qualities of Buddha and Je Tsongkhapa   142

Colophon   145

APPENDICES

Appendix I: 151
Dedicating the Illusory Body as Ganachakra:
Promoting the Experience of Means and Wisdom,
Wealth of the Ganden Practice Lineage
by Kyabje Phabongka Dechen Nyingpo

Appendix II: 167
Offering Ganachakra in Connection with the
Yoga of the Profound Path of Chöd
written and compiled by Kyabje Zong Rinpoche Losang Tsöndru

Appendix III: 193
Umapa Pawo Dorje's Commentary on Chöd
as Taught by Venerable Manjushri

Appendix IV: 201
Prayer for the Flourishing of Je Tsongkhapa's Teachings
by Gungthang Tenpai Dronme

Appendix V: 203
The Sages' Melodious Song of Truth:
Nonpartisan Prayer for the Flourishing of Buddha's Teachings
by His Holiness the Fourteenth Dalai Lama

Notes   209

Acknowledgments

We of Zong Labrang, Gaden Mahayana University, South India, would like to express our immense gratitude for the hard work, time, and dedicated effort contributed to this work by Tenzin Paksam, Julia and Keith Milton, Geshe Lobsang Tsultrim of Zong Labrang, and David Molk in particular, for acting as chief editor. We pray that the effort and faith shown by them will spread the message of this book throughout the world.

Wednesday, July 19, 2006

Recordings Available

Two CD recordings of texts translated in the appendices to this book are available from Snow Lion Publications. They are:

(1) *Dedicating the Illusory Body as Ganachakra: Promoting the Experience of Means and Wisdom, Wealth of the Ganden Practice Lineage,* by Kyabje Phabongka Dechen Nyingpo, chanted in English to the Tibetan melodies with damaru and bone trumpet by the translator, David Molk,

and

(2) *Offering Ganachakra in Connection with the Yoga of the Profound Path of Chöd,* written and compiled by Kyabje Zong Rinpoche Losang Tsöndru, chanted by the translator, David Molk, in English to the Tibetan melodies with damaru and bell.

For ordering information, please check our website. The complete Snow Lion catalog is also available online: http://www.snowlionpub.com.

Snow Lion Publications
P.O. Box 643
Ithaca, NY 14851 USA
Telephone: 800-950-0313 (orders only), or 607-273-8519
Fax: 607-273-8508
www.snowlionpub.com

Kyabje Zong Rinpoche Losang Tsöndru

Kyabje Zong Rinpoche

A Biographical Profile

Zongtrul Jetsun Losang Tsöndru Thubten Gyaltsen—or Venerable Kyabje Zong Rinpoche, as he is known to countless ordained and lay disciples—was born in 1905 in the village of Nangsang in the Kham province of eastern Tibet. His father and both his grandfathers were *ngakpa*, tantric practitioners of the Nyingma tradition, and two previous incarnations of Kyabje Dorje Chang ("Vajradhara, Lord of Refuge," as Kyabje Zong Rinpoche was also known) had taken birth within the Zong-go family: Zongtrul Phuntsok Chöpel and Zongtrul Tenpa Chöpel (1836-1899).

It is said that when Zongtrul Tenpa Chöpel was about to pass away, his niece's husband came to visit him and persuaded him to extend his life. Later, when Zongtrul Rinpoche was again about to end his earthly existence, his niece's husband made the same request. This time the master refused, but on being asked to take rebirth within the same family, he gave his relative three apricots. He told him to eat one himself, to give the second to his niece, and to plant the last one in front of their house. "When the tree first begins to bear fruit," Rinpoche said, "I will once again take rebirth in the Zong-go family!" Five years later, Zongtrul Rinpoche fulfilled his promise.

In 1916, following his recognition as the new incarnation of Zongtrul Tenpa Chöpel, the eleven-year-old Zong Rinpoche made the long and arduous journey to central Tibet.[1] He came to study at Ganden Monastery, one of Tibet's great monastic universities, forty kilometers (twenty-five miles) northeast of Lhasa. Upon his arrival, his appointed attendant offered the young tulku some sobering advice. "From now on," he said, "you need to study hard, because you will not be respected back at your home monastery if you don't do well. My duty is to earn whatever I can to support your Geshe ceremony." This was no small feat. The occasion of a student earning his Geshe degree was marked by a feast offering[2] and a personal donation to the entire population of monks, which at that time numbered around 2,500. Unfortunately, the attendant did not live to see Rinpoche complete his degree. When Zong Rinpoche entered Ganden's Shartse College, the fourteen-year-old Venerable Kyabje Trijang Rinpoche (who was to become one of the main tutors of His Holiness the XIV Dalai Lama) guided the new student by taking him through his first lesson in elementary dialectics. He was later to become Zong Rinpoche's chief mentor.

Although recognized by everyone as a reincarnate lama, Zong Rinpoche did not enjoy the privileges accorded to modern-day tulkus. He had no benefactor to support him, nor was he interested in finding one. The young monk lived a spartan existence. Instead of a table from which to read the scriptures, he made do with an empty tea box supported by bricks. He was completely focused on his studies, which he pursued with unfailing courage and diligence. He seemed disinterested in food or drink, surviving on a very simple diet. With his humble lifestyle and shabby robes, often loose and torn from the physicality of the debate ground, he looked like any other boy from the remote province of Kham who had been fortunate enough to attend this prestigious monastic university.

Zong Rinpoche received his full ordination from the Thirteenth Dalai Lama at the Potala Palace, and soon after that, during even his first year at the monastery, his teachers began to see in the young lama the makings of a talented debater. During an all-night debating session on Pramana between Ganden's twin colleges of Shartse and Jangtse, he surprised the senior Jangtse scholars with the depth of his debating skills. During a similar session a year later, he advanced a debate on the opening verse of *Pramanavarttika*, the foremost dissertation on Buddhist logic by the famed seventh-century Indian logician Acharya Dharmakirti. Zong Rinpoche's performance led the famous Geshe "Amdo" Sherab Gyatso to remark, "There would not be a worthier debate on this subject even if Dharmakirti himself were here in person!" Along with his formidable skill in debate,

Zong Rinpoche possessed a fertile intelligence and great powers of reten-
tion, and his name gradually became known throughout the three great
Gelug monasteries of central Tibet: Ganden, Drepung, and Sera.

At the age of twenty-five, Zong Rinpoche was examined along with a
group of elite students from Ganden, Sera, and Drepung to see who would
qualify for the highest rank of Geshe Lharampa. The exams were held at
the Norbulingka, the summer palace of His Holiness the Dalai Lama. The
Great Thirteenth Dalai Lama, who was present during one of the examinations, offered warm applause after Zong Rinpoche's performance and
remarked, "Zong Lama has studied excellently. He deserves the first or
second rank Geshe Lharampa this year!" Soon after qualifying with the
highest honors of Lharampa Geshe, Zong Rinpoche enjoyed an equally
successful examination at Gyütö Tantric College. These achievements
firmly established his reputation as an accomplished scholar.

In 1930, Rinpoche participated in the final debate examinations of the
Great Prayer Festival, Mönlam Chenmo, at the Jokhang Cathedral in Lhasa.
Here, the Geshe candidates engaged in three debate sessions a day for over
a week. The topics were the five major Buddhist subjects: *Pramana* (Logic
and Cognition), *Paramita* (Perfections), *Madhyamaka* (Middle Way Philos-
ophy), *Abhidharma* (Phenomenology), and *Vinaya* (Ethical Codes and Conduct). Many years later, a number of former abbots reminisced about being
young students at these debate sessions, seated behind rows of highly educated senior monks. They recalled overhearing the senior monks whisper-
ing among themselves that this Zong Rinpoche was a brilliant and gifted
scholar who was bold enough to challenge anyone in debate. Some of them
even decided to leave the debate ground altogether rather than risk the
humiliation of losing to a junior monk.

In the mid-1930's Zong Rinpoche became deeply influenced by Madhyamaka. His analysis and meditation in this area perfected his understanding of the ultimate intent of the Buddha and enabled him to develop
genuine insight into the relationship between emptiness and the interdependence of all phenomena. These convictions burned within him, finally
leading him to make the decision to return to his home province and dedicate the rest of his life to the practice of Tantra in conjunction with the
insights of Nagarjuna.

However, this was not to be. One day, Thepo Rinpoche called him to his quarters and told him, "Put aside thoughts of returning home or anywhere else. Stay comfortably here in the monastery!" A few months later Reteng Rinpoche, the Regent of Tibet, appointed the thirty-three year old Zong Rinpoche to the position of abbot of Ganden Shartse. The influence of Zong Rinpoche's term as abbot is still felt today. As well as reaching new heights of scholarship, Ganden Shartse became an outstanding example of monastic discipline, something that Zong Rinpoche held to be of vital importance. He also inspired a strong interest in Tantra, Chöd, and monastic ritual, and significantly improved the monastery's administrative structure. Having personally experienced the difficulties faced by its poorer members, Zong Rinpoche introduced reforms that went a long way toward improving their situation.

After serving as the monastery's abbot for over nine years, Zong Rinpoche resigned from his seat in 1946 and went on a long pilgrimage to Tsari, southeastern Tibet. From that time onwards, intermittent reports were heard of Rinpoche's removing people's difficulties and obstacles through low-key demonstrations of tantric power. The well-known Geshe Rinpoche Tenzin Chöpel, whose eyesight was so damaged that he was unable to walk unassisted, invited Zong Rinpoche for a visit in the hope of receiving a cure for his condition. After Zong Rinpoche had conducted several eye-cleansing rituals, he was able to dispense with his cane and walk on his own.

In many areas of Tibet, as well as at Ganden and its adjacent lower lands of Dechen, Lamdo, Cheka, and Zibuk, Zong Rinpoche quietly and successfully subdued the powerful local spirits so that they ceased causing harm and disturbances. Fields, plantations, and orchards were seen to increase their yields after he had visited and said the necessary prayers, and his ability to bring about and stop rain and hailstorms became legendary.

In the aftermath of the suppression of his homeland in 1959, and after repeated appeals from his disciples and students all over the country who were concerned for his safety, Zong Rinpoche left Tibet and sought asylum in India. In the remote settlement of Buxa in the Indian state of Assam on the Bhutanese border, he joined the surviving members of Ganden, Drepung, and Sera, as well as monks from other Tibetan monasteries.

Although they were now safe from persecution, the monks found it difficult to adapt to the extreme tropical climate. The older monks especially suffered greatly in the heat, and many died of tuberculosis and other diseases, thus further decimating the population of learned Tibetan Buddhist practitioners.

Amidst all these hardships and challenges, Zong Rinpoche gave countless teachings, and in doing so, rekindled the flame of Buddha's doctrine in exile. For the refugee monks, Rinpoche's inspired commentaries on Buddhadharma offered a revitalizing hope and relief from complete despair. In 1965, acting upon a request from His Holiness the XIV Dalai Lama, Zong Rinpoche took a position as the director of the newly formed Tibetan Schools Teachers Training Program in Mussoorie (north-west India), overseeing fifty-eight scholars from all the major traditions of Tibetan Buddhism. This educational nucleus proved crucial to the success of the fledgling Tibetan refugee settlements and had far-reaching benefits for all the Tibetan schools that were subsequently established.

Two years later, His Holiness the Dalai Lama appointed him to be the first principal of the new Central Institute of Tibetan Higher Studies at Sarnath, Varanasi, India. On a visit to Thubten Dhargye Ling Buddhist Center in California in December 1983, Kyabje Zong Rinpoche recalled the meeting with His Holiness in 1967:

> In Buxa, the monastic community came to hear of a prophecy by the State Oracle that the life of His Holiness the Dalai Lama was in danger. Everyone became very alarmed, and I was asked by many to go to Dharamsala to request His Holiness' long life.

Zong Rinpoche arrived in Dharamsala at the time of Tibetan New Year and waited for His Holiness in the audience hall. When His Holiness arrived, he greeted Zong Rinpoche by fondly taking hold of his beard in the playful manner he often displays with those closest to him, and then took him aside.

> His Holiness already knew why I had come to Dharamsala. He told me, "You became anxious, but I won't die, so just relax!" When he

said this to me I was so moved that I suddenly burst into tears, and my happiness knew no bounds.

Zong Rinpoche went on to describe how His Holiness told him that he was happy that Rinpoche had accepted the position of principal. Zong Rinpoche replied that he had felt it his duty to take the position even though he wondered if he was up to the task due to his age and health problems that affected his feet and respiration. "His Holiness mentioned to me that age doesn't matter, that it can be minimized, but I didn't have the courage to ask him what he meant by this. When I returned to Buxa, however, it was exactly as His Holiness had said. I really became younger. I no longer needed my walking stick, nor did I have any more respiratory problems."

After retiring from public life in 1971, Zong Rinpoche took the opportunity to spend more of his time in deep spiritual practices. During these quiet years, he would occasionally give highly inspiring teachings, which often contained instructions on practical aspects of Vajrayana. In fact, whenever he taught, Rinpoche always placed great emphasis on the practical aspect of religious activity.

His humanity, scholarship, and spiritual realization were not to be confined to Tibetan society, however. As the years passed, his fame spread abroad, and invitations poured in requesting him to come to the West. Kyabje Zong Rinpoche took three trips outside of India. The first was in 1978, at the request of Lama Thubten Yeshe. During these tours, Rinpoche visited Dharma centers in Europe, the U.S., and Canada. He was always fascinated with how things worked, and was very skillful with his hands. A student recalled how, on a visit to the Tower of London, he "captivated a crowd of tourists with his detailed and accurate explanation of the workings of an ancient blunderbuss!" In response to requests by Western students, he lectured on the full range of Buddhist thought and practice, and gave many personal interviews. Those who came into contact with him were deeply moved and inspired by his warmth and wisdom. One of his Western students recalls him saying to her at their first meeting, "Do not think that I am anything special. Think that it is by the power of your karma that you have the good fortune to meet the Dharma."

In 1981, Zong Rinpoche's teacher, Kyabje Trijang Rinpoche, was taken seriously ill at his residence in Mundgod. Rinpoche describes their last meeting. "Just before I was about to leave for the United States we had lunch together. 'In terms of our friendship, you are my oldest friend,' he told me, 'and in terms of guru-disciple relationship, you are my most senior disciple.'" Kyabje Zong Rinpoche often mentioned to his resident students, as an instruction on guru devotion, that he had never harbored a negative thought for his teacher, Kyabje Trijang Rinpoche, for even a single instant. "Again Kyabje Trijang Rinpoche remarked, 'You are my most trusted and loved student.' He took my hand and placed it on his forehead and I realized he had a fever. He asked me to look at his hands, and I saw that there was hardly any flesh on them. I was suddenly struck by a deep sorrow. We touched foreheads and his parting words were: 'Anyway, we will meet again soon!' I was unable to speak any more and had to leave." Kyabje Trijang Rinpoche passed away that year at the age of eighty-one—the same age, Zong Rinpoche noted in one of his talks, that Shakyamuni Buddha had reached when he entered parinirvana.

Kyabje Zong Rinpoche's penetrating insights into everything he taught had a profound effect on all who heard them. His teachings, they observed, were not just intellectual, for he seemed to draw upon an inexhaustible fountain of direct personal experience. His listeners responded by introducing great positive changes in their lives. Zong Rinpoche will primarily be remembered in the West as one of the first Tibetan masters to introduce Western students to the most profound aspects of Tibetan Buddhism. His skill as a teacher revealed itself in his ability to adapt his teaching methods to the views and temperament of the modern mind. He was known for his unique narrative style that was simultaneously highly engaging and absolutely straightforward. Kyabje Zong Rinpoche retained these wonderful qualities until the very last days of his life. When he passed away, he left behind the legacy of an energetic, compelling, direct and highly accomplished spiritual master.

KYABJE ZONG RINPOCHE'S PASSING

In 1983, Kyabje Zong Rinpoche made his third trip to the West and embarked on a teaching tour that took him to England, Canada, the U.S.,

Switzerland, Spain, France, Germany, Italy and Austria. In June 1984, fervent and repeated requests by his students in India caused Rinpoche to cancel the remaining three months of his European schedule and return to his home at Ganden Monastery, by then reestablished in Mundgod in southern India. The following month, Zong Rinpoche gave pith instructions on the Hayagriva Tantra, followed by the Chittamani Tara initiation, and a long life empowerment for all the Tibetans in Mundgod's refugee community. Shortly after the last of these teachings, he arranged an elaborate offering ceremony for the Dharma Protectors. After a few days of rituals, the students at Zong Labrang, Rinpoche's residential compound, reported that Zong Rinpoche had fallen ill with a high fever. Although his doctors gave him the best medical care, his condition did not improve.

All of the twenty-one students who lived with him in his residence and everyone in the monastery offered numerous long life prayers, imploring Rinpoche to recover. The monastic Dharma Protector in particular begged him in the name of the Buddha's doctrine and all sentient beings to regain his health and live for many more years. In the event that this was not to be, the Protector added, Rinpoche should at least prolong his life until the reincarnation of Venerable Kyabje Trijang Rinpoche was legitimately determined.

As the news of Zong Rinpoche's ailing physical condition spread, delegates began to arrive to pay their respects and offer long life requests and ceremonies. Visitors from Drepung and Sera monasteries, including representatives of the two tantric colleges, Gyutö and Gyume, and all of the incarnate lamas of these great Buddhist institutions, came to offer long life prayers. Four months later, at the beginning of November 1984, Rinpoche suddenly declared, "I do not have any of my former illness." Once again, in apparently good health, he resumed his daily routine, and, upon requests from the monastery and other communities, presided over the ceremony to determine the new incarnation of Kyabje Trijang Rinpoche.

Prior to his illness, and again during this time, some of his attendants noticed that Rinpoche engaged in the self-empowerment rituals of Heruka Chakrasamvara, Vajrayogini, and Chittamani Tara over long periods of time, and they observed him in "unusual states of absorption," as one of them later described it. Rinpoche became increasingly gentle as each day gave way to the next. He summoned his resident students in groups as well as individually and offered them profound and intimate advice. He made observations on a number of topics, including Dharma centers in the West. At one time, he remarked to his personal attendant, Tenzin Wangchuk, with his characteristic directness, "I cannot bear this hot weather. I would like to be in the cool. Let me see for a few days… I might get used to it. If I can bear it I will remain. If not I might leave." At another time, he said to his students, "You have been so kind to me. I thank you all for the services you have rendered me during my recent illness. How pleasant it is here, to be in this house. What could be more comfortable than to be surrounded by my own students?"

Rinpoche normally awoke at three o'clock in the morning and finished his daily meditation before dawn. In the early morning hours of November fifteenth, exactly two weeks after his recovery, Zong Rinpoche repeatedly asked a young resident, "Did the dawn break?" When the answer was negative, Rinpoche remarked, "It seems to be taking a long time for dawn to arrive today." Rinpoche touched the right side of his chest and complained of a minor pain, but his discomfort seemed to subside as the new day dawned beneath a clear sky.

The day, marking Buddha's descent into this world after returning from the Celestial Realm of Indra, would come to strike everyone with immense sadness and grief. But now, in the tranquil morning air, the newly risen sun bathed Rinpoche's eastern-facing residence in glory, and shafts of early morning light flooded his reception room. He ate a hearty breakfast, which made everyone very happy. As his attendant removed the tray he softly remarked, "This was appetizing, completely satisfying and excellent. You have been extremely kind."

At that time, someone delivered a large color photograph of Kyabje Trijang Rinpoche's stupa sent by one of Rinpoche's Italian students. Taking the picture in his hands, Rinpoche asked his attendant, Tenzin Wangchuk, if he understood the significance of the gift. "If you don't," he explained, "it implies that you should build such a stupa. Can you construct something like this? Even if you cannot build a traditional one, my students will build a stupa in the future with their wisdom and practice!"

Tenzin Wangchuk told Rinpoche that he had called a medical doctor from the Dueguling Tibetan Resettlement Hospital half a mile away to give Rinpoche a check-up. It was shortly after nine o'clock in the morning when the doctor arrived. Rinpoche stood up and walked from his bedroom into his sitting room, saying that he would like to sit in an upright posture. The sitting room was Rinpoche's favorite room. The door led to his garden, and he liked to watch the sun rise from its eastern window.

During his illness, Rinpoche had generally relied on someone to support him while he walked, but today he told his students emphatically, "Nobody needs to hold me. I can go on my own." He once again declared to those around him that he was no longer ill, and left the bedroom in his usual brisk manner. In the sitting room, Rinpoche stretched out his legs and let the doctor examine him. After the examination, the doctor told the students that he could detect no serious illness, only that Rinpoche was rather weak and could use some glucose. However, as the doctor didn't have any glucose with him, he sent his assistant back to his clinic to fetch some.

When the students entered the room a few minutes later, their beloved Teacher had left them for another realm. As he had prophesied, Rinpoche did not die in hospital, in pain, or from a serious illness. Those around him were amazed how Rinpoche's body remained as if in a deep sleep, without losing luster or color. It was clear that their teacher was in a most subtle state of mind, embracing the meditation of clear light. He was eighty years old.

As news of Kyabje Zong Rinpoche's passing spread through the monastery, the first reaction was one of shock and disbelief. Although his supreme spiritual accomplishment meant that he was not subject to death in the usual sense, Rinpoche's passing was completely unexpected, and rendered all the more devastating by its suddenness. The monastic community was plunged into anguish and despair. Amidst a sea of eyes glistening with tears, the news was officially declared in the main prayer halls, where the entire community of Shartse and Jangtse colleges had congregated to offer Ganachakra in Rinpoche's memory.

The Representative Officer of His Holiness the Dalai Lama came to offer his condolences, and was soon followed by delegates from Drepung Monastery and others who streamed into Rinpoche's residence compound. In his rooms, last rites began the same day, with Vajrayogini self-initiation presided over by Venerable Kyabje Zemey Rinpoche, foremost among Zong Rinpoche's innumerable disciples; Khen Rinpoche Jhampa Yeshe, the abbot of Shartse; and Khensur Losang Tenpa, the former abbot of Gyutö Tantric College, along with other highly realized disciples.

As dusk fell, the whole area of Ganden Monastery was illuminated with butter lamps. For six hours, the night resounded with thousands of monks reciting the *Essence of Eloquence*, Lama Tsongkhapa's masterpiece of Sutrayana. To complete the cremation rites on the basis of the Vajrasattva Tantra, these recitations were followed the next day with the senior tulkus performing the complete self-empowerment of Heruka Chakrasamvara's Body Mandala. In the evening, all the monks of Ganden Shartse recited the root texts of Maitreya's *Ornament of Realization* and Chandrakirti's *Guide to the Middle Way*. Meanwhile, the monks of Ganden Jangste also gathered at Zong Labrang and recited Guhyasamaja sadhanas.

On Saturday, the third day after Rinpoche's passing, Kyabje Zemey Rinpoche and other high lamas gathered to conduct a self-initiation of Chittamani Tara, and the monks of Ganden Shartse, who had completed a Yamantaka retreat, conducted the self-initiation of Yamantaka. From the day Rinpoche had passed away the air had remained so still that barely a single leaf had rustled in the garden, but around three o'clock the weather suddenly changed and a strong wind came up, violently blowing the dust from the ground into the sky. When the wind subsided, word spread that Zong Rinpoche had arisen from the Clear Light state and had ascended into the enlightened realm. Residents of Mundgod also reported feeling land tremors before and after Rinpoche's passing. Countless numbers of people, including abbots, high-ranking lamas, and geshes from all three monastic universities, came to pay their respects and take an active part in the rituals. Everyone recited the prayer for the swift arrival of Rinpoche's reincarnation that Zemey Rinpoche had composed two days after his passing.

That evening Kyabje Zemey Rinpoche led Rinpoche's close disciples in bathing and dressing Rinpoche's body in full initiation costume. Bell and vajra were placed in his hands, and his body was laid in a richly arrayed wooden casket, which had been made into a palanquin. One by one, monks from the great monasteries filed in to pay their respects. By this time, the eastern sitting room was open to the public so people could receive the final blessing from Rinpoche's sacred corporeal form.

Surrounding the eastern room of the Labrang, the monks of Ganden Shartse formed three groups. The first group began to recite the root text of Acharya Dharmakirti's *Logic in Four Volumes*. The second group recited the Abhidharma text composed by Acharya Vasubandhu, and the third group recited *Guide to the Bodhisattva's Way of Life*, by Acharya Shantideva. At the same time, the monks of Ganden Jangtse gathered to recite Maitreya's *Ornament of Realization* and Chandrakirti's *Guide to the Middle Way* as the Ganden Shartse monks had done the evening before. As the junior and senior monks surrounding Rinpoche's residence chanted these texts, the high lamas gathered inside to perform tantric rituals.

At eight o'clock on the morning of the fourth day, Sunday, the eighteenth of November, the palanquin slowly emerged from Rinpoche's residence. Held aloft by his close students under a revolving parasol, it wound its way ceremoniously toward the cremation hearth that had been especially prepared within the compound. Throngs of monks, nuns, and laypeople, including many schoolchildren bearing flowers, lined the path amidst flying banners and the sounds of cymbals and conch shells. Amongst the mourners were some of Rinpoche's disciples who had traveled from Europe and North America as soon as they had heard of his passing.

Those who were present during these days witnessed many unusual signs. On the third day, just before the cremation hearth was lit, seven Indian ascetics clad in new saffron robes and leading a loaded elephant walked into the compound. When asked what they were doing there, they replied that this day marked a very auspicious occasion, and asked for an offering. Tenzin Wangchuk offered them bananas and money, and they left, satisfied. It was an unprecedented event, and everyone remarked that it was a very auspicious sign. Later, when monks asked the local villagers about the elephant, they couldn't find anyone who had seen it. During the cremation, the community recited a multitude of prayers and texts, made tsog offerings, and performed rituals. Students of the monastery voluntarily spent entire nights before the cremation hearth reciting key sutras and tantras.

In Tibetan tradition, the elephant is often compared to a bull. When the reincarnation of Kyabje Zong Rinpoche was born on May 27, 1985, in the year of the Bull or the Ox, and the reincarnation of Kyabje Trijang Rinpoche was confirmed by His Holiness the Dalai Lama that same year, it became clear that the appearance of the elephant and the ascetics had had a definite significance.

The twenty-fourth of November was the night of the full moon. It was one of the days that Rinpoche had circled in his diary before his death, and so it was on this morning that the members of Zong Labrang opened the cremation hearth. Lying among Rinpoche's ashes they found his skull unburned and completely intact. Zong Rinpoche's previous incarnation, Zongtrul Tenpa Chöpel, who had died in 1899, had also left his skull intact. That relic, which bears the Tibetan syllable AH, is kept to this day at Zong Rinpoche's residence as a treasure of faith and honor.

Two hollow pans had been placed, one atop the other, in the lower part of the hearth. The rim of the upper pan was cemented to the inner walls of the hearth, while the lower pan was turned as a lid over the sand mandala beneath. When the cremation hearth was opened, a large quantity of relic pills were found between the two pans. Finally, when the lower pan was removed, everyone present, including some of Zong Rinpoche's Western disciples, saw in the sand mandala two unmistakable footprints of an infant, complete with heels and toes. The discovery of these extraordinary signs made everyone feel great peace, reaffirming their faith in their Teacher, and assuring them that his return would be swift.

A week before Rinpoche passed away, he had had a survey conducted around the compound of Zong Labrang and had asked his attendant, Tenzin Wangchuk, to remove a pile of dirt and concrete from a specific area in the yard. The supposed reason was that this area was to be used as a place for the monks to do physical exercise. However, in reality, Rinpoche meant for this place to become the site of the stupa-like hearth in which his body would be cremated, and this spot would remain a cremation site thereafter.

Also, some time before his passing, Kyabje Zong Rinpoche had circled three dates in his diary. The first was the date that he rose from the Clear Light state. The second was the day of the cremation. The third was the day the cremation hearth was opened. This made it very convenient for the disciples to plan and conduct the traditional arrangements, but the real message is, of course, that Rinpoche had gone beyond ordinary death and rebirth. His last extraordinary deeds demonstrated a fully controlled, fearless death. They teach us that one day, everything must come to an end. Those present were indelibly impressed with the knowledge that practice and effort can enable one to completely transcend death. Thus, the life of Kyabje Zong Rinpoche became a teaching on how to live meaningfully and die well.

Zong Rinpoche's reincarnation was born in India, in the Kullu Valley, revered by Hindus as a sacred site of Lord Shiva and his consort, Parvati. The Kullu Valley is also revered by Tibetan lamas as one of the twenty-four sites sacred to Heruka Chakrasamvara.

Zong Rinpoche's "precious tomb stupa," or *dung-ten*, was completed in 1986 by members of Zong Labrang, with contributions from a number of Rinpoche's disciples. It stands five feet high, is covered with precious stones and metals, and is filled with relics and holy objects. Today, it stands in a place of honor in the center of the Zong Labrang prayer room.

Introduction: The "Sacred Cutting" of Chöd

Mind amidst the eight petals, in avadhuti,
Free of all projections, clear light's bliss goddess,
The magical Lady of Five Lights' beautiful play
Displays inconceivable yuganaddha!

How pleasant, the profound, most secret swift path!
How blissful, this gathering with pure samaya!
In glory of ganachakra's blissful union,
This connection transcends meeting and parting!
— Kyabje Trijang Dorje Chang[3]

THE FOUNDER of the Ganden tradition,[4] Je Tsongkhapa Losang Dragpa, in his *Commentary on the Profound Path of Chöd*,[5] said,

All Mahayana training is included in *lojong*,
And all Mahayana Dharma is included in Chöd.

Thus, Chöd is nothing less than one of the most sublime expressions of Buddhadharma. Originating out of the enlightened Tibetan Lady Machig Labdrön's[6] realization of Buddha's Sutra and Tantra teachings, it was highly treasured by Kyabje Zong Rinpoche and the lineage gurus of the Ganden Oral Tradition. Chöd is, in essence, the main path to full enlightenment, the Great Mother from whom all enlightened beings are born. *Chöd* means "cutting"; that is, cutting through the misconception of self that is at the very root of samsara. Buddha frees beings from suffering by helping them realize the actual nature of their own existence. It is the realization of True Paths, the Perfection of Wisdom, which eradicates the ignorance obscuring the minds of beings.

Buddha said, "Nonseeing is the highest sacred seeing." Similarly speaking, the "cutting" of Chöd is sacred, because it severs the root of suffering and leads to highest enlightenment, and it is a "noncutting," because it is an illusory cutting in which, ultimately, no agent, object, or action of cutting can be found. With its special emphasis on the sacrifice of self for others, Chöd is an extraordinary form of *lojong*, mind training, indispensable to attainment of full enlightenment. Chöd practice also provides a field for action in which the full resources of Buddha's teachings can be brought to bear on the healing of beings throughout the human and spirit worlds.

TAKING VAST SCRIPTURAL LEARNING AS PERSONAL ADVICE

In order to practice Chöd, one must receive the initiation known as the "Sky-Opener." From Khedrub Chöje (also known as Khedrub Chenpo Zhönu Drub), Je Tsongkhapa received the Chöd lineages that can be traced back through Machig Labdrön and Padampa Sangye to Buddha Shakyamuni. Je Tsongkhapa also received teachings on Chöd directly from Manjushri. This visionary lineage is known as the Ganden Oral Lineage of Chöd. A "Dakini" oral lineage is also practiced in Gelug.[7] Je Tsongkhapa passed the Chöd to only one of his disciples, Togden Jampel Gyatso, who was the principal holder of his Tantric Mahamudra lineage as well. The first personal advice Togden Jampel Gyatso ever received from Je Tsongkhapa was:

> In order to realize the essence of Dharma practice, it is necessary to obtain understanding in the complete path; and in order for that to happen, one has to study, using stainless reasoning, the [two] traditions of the Mahayana. Only in this way can one properly differentiate the true path from the nonpath. Therefore, you must study all the traditional subjects, beginning with logic and so forth.[8]

Engaging in maximum study for the sole purpose of integrating it into meditation and yogic practice strongly characterizes the Ganden tradition. Je Tsongkhapa says in his *Commentary on the Profound Path of Chöd,*

> Although you may have studied the Chöd literature extensively, and done a lot of teaching, debate, and writing, if you don't subdue your own mind and are content with a scholarly, literal reading of the text, having studied Dharma but not put it into practice, then what is the use of studying Sutra and Tantra?

Reflecting on such qualities, I write from our temple-hermitage, Ganden Samten Ling, which overlooks the southern coastline of Big Sur, California, and which is dedicated to Kyabje Zong Rinpoche. It is the greatest honor of my life to have been asked to write this introduction to the life and work of Kyabje Zong Rinpoche, and to Chöd in the Ganden tradition. My soulmate Gayle and I were among many Western students who had the opportunity to receive Chöd empowerment and teachings from the late Kyabje Zong Rinpoche, a giant of the past generation of Tibetan Buddhist masters. I was irresistibly drawn to Chöd's hypnotically melodious practices, and, after chanting them in Tibetan for years, eventually created and set to the blessed melodies the English translations for practice that are included in appendices I and II of this book. It is only through the late Kyabje Zong Rinpoche's pioneering effort that we have had the opportunity to encounter this practice, and it is, again, only thanks to the kindness of his present incarnation[9] that we have had the opportunity to create this present volume. It is intended to facilitate practice for those who have received empowerment, the best way to show the Guru our gratitude. I pray it may become part of the "wisdom stupa"[10] that Kyabje Zong Rinpoche predicted his students would create.

KYABJE ZONG RINPOCHE AND HIS PREVIOUS LIVES

Prior to Kyabje Zong Rinpoche's life, the practice of Chöd in the Ganden tradition was at the point of extinction. Even though Chöd remained an innermost essence practice of the Ganden tradition lineage masters, its outward practice was largely forbidden at major Gelugpa monasteries starting in the 1930s.[11] More generally, the decimation of the Tibetan population and its culture that occurred as a result of the Chinese invasion and occupation of Tibet was also responsible for the dwindling strength of Chöd practice. Kyabje Zong Rinpoche encouraged renewed practice of Chöd at Ganden Monastery in Tibet when he was abbot of Ganden Shartse and later propagated Chöd in the Tibetan exile community in India. At Ganden Monastery and other Gelugpa monasteries, the practice of Chöd is once again strong.

Kyabje Zong Rinpoche and the Ganden tradition's qualities are so vast and multifaceted that no one person could adequately describe them. As in Atisha's Kadampa tradition, practitioners in the Ganden tradition keep their inner qualities hidden, like a lamp inside a pot. Kyabje Zong Rinpoche never promoted himself. He refrained from giving teachings on guru devotion in the West for years out of a concern that people might misinterpret it to mean that he was seeking offerings. Still, as it is said,

> Though the highest hide their qualities,
> They illuminate the whole world!
> Even if you cover a flower bouquet,
> The sweet fragrance reaches everywhere!

It was impossible for Kyabje Zong Rinpoche's qualities not to shine forth. His mere presence affected people profoundly. When he was young he would not accept special treatment as a tulku, but studied as an ordinary monk and completed his training, intending only to devote his life to yogic practice. Yet he was called upon to become abbot of Ganden Monastery, and the spiritual guide for an entire generation of Tibetans. He was fearlessly outspoken in maintaining purity of Buddhadharma, and just as rigorous in his own self-discipline.

We once came across a large collection of interviews with Tibetan tulkus. In each of the interviews the lamas described their previous incarnations. Seeing Kyabje Zong Rinpoche's name in the table of contents, we turned the pages, wondering if we might learn something of Rinpoche's previous lives. Instead we found a virtual indictment of the entire tulku system. He said nothing at all about his own previous incarnations. The gist of what Rinpoche said in the interview was that attachment between lamas and their disciples sometimes played too strong a role in the search for and identification of their reincarnations. Rinpoche would sometimes say that, if he were asked for his preference with regard to a teacher, he would choose a highly trained geshe over a recognized tulku who had not attained a similar level of education. He said on another occasion that if a child appeared and claimed to be the Zong Lama after he himself had passed away, the child should not be believed. "Throw ashes in his mouth, and just give him Dharma books to study, but nothing else!" he said.

Kyabje Zong Rinpoche was a consummate master of Sutra and Tantra, eminently qualified for practice of Chöd. In the Ganden tradition, Chöd is viewed as quite advanced, a kind of "graduate level" practice, to be most fully practiced after having completed study of both Sutra and Tantra. While inner practice of Chöd is pervasive in Mahayana, dealing as it does with realization of conventional and ultimate bodhichitta, the outer practice was kept carefully hidden. It is a mark of Kyabje Zong Rinpoche's confidence of realization that, at the request of His Holiness the Dalai Lama, he was willing to cross cultural boundaries and teach Western students the most profound secrets of Tantra and Chöd. Laying bare the path to enlightenment, he urged purity of practice and inspired disciples through his unique example.

In the Ganden tradition it is considered ideal to maintain Pratimoksha discipline outwardly, while inwardly engaging in the bodhisattva's heroic sacrifice of self for other, and secretly practicing Highest Yoga Tantra to manifest enlightenment swiftly. Heruka-Vajravarahi Tantra, and, in particular, Vajravarahi in her outer, inner and secret (Tröma Nagmo) forms, is central to Chöd practice. The teachings and actions of Kyabje Zong Rinpoche made it abundantly clear that he had completed this Tantric path. He was widely held to *be* Heruka-Vajravarahi. He was an embodiment of the complete Buddhadharma, whom any practitioner would have been awed to have had as his or her guru.

Kyabje Zong Rinpoche never watered down or sugarcoated the teachings to make them more palatable, nor would he pretend that the spiritual path was easy and required no effort. He would often say that a subject he was explaining could only be fully understood by the highly educated geshes. Yet by his very willingness to come to the West and reveal the complete path, including Tantric practice, he empowered students with the confidence that they, too, could accomplish the spiritual path. He said, "In the beginning take your Guru as your teacher, in the middle take the scriptures as your teacher, in the end take your own mind as your teacher."

One of the teachings Rinpoche taught without any sugarcoating was the doctrine of reincarnation. In the strongly materialistic, "modern" world, people sometimes have difficulty understanding reincarnation, or cannot accept it at all, and so some teachers make their instructions more palatable by asserting that there is no way to be sure that past and future lives exist, or that it is not important to think about. Rinpoche never diluted the Dharma in such a manner. Just as a wise person does not begin a journey without planning far ahead, Rinpoche maintained that in order to receive the fullest benefit of Dharma practice, we would have to realize that reincarnation did exist, and that we were merely temporary visitors who would be moving on from the "guest house" of our bodies.

Once he recounted questioning several young tulkus about how they had arrived in their mothers' wombs. Lacking words to describe it, one child put his hands together and made an undulating downward, diving sort of motion that Rinpoche took great delight in demonstrating to us. There seems to be ample evidence of reincarnation, especially from the mouths of children, in every society throughout the world. Buddha's teachings *do* present logical reasoning establishing the existence of past and future lives, but in order to gain actual experience of that logic, one must have understanding of the nature of mind. Kyabje Zong Rinpoche taught in great detail about the nature of mind and the process of death, intermediate state and rebirth, even instructing us as to how one could navigate and transcend that process with complete freedom and control just as he did. A great being incarnating in the world out of compassion for beings, he once remarked, during a break in an offering ceremony, "There's no time to change bodies now!"

The lineage speaks of twenty-five known previous incarnations of Kyabje Zong Rinpoche, reaching back to the time of Buddha Shakyamuni. I was given the names of nine or so, including the two mentioned at the beginning of the biographical profile, and another one that was not fully identified. Here I'll mention six, plus two more that came to light as a result of my own research.

At the time of Buddha, he took birth as the Bodhisattva Matiprabha, Light of Discernment, about whom I have no further information. Perhaps he was present when the Brahmin youth, who in the future would take birth as Je Tsongkhapa, made an offering of a crystal mala to Buddha Shakyamuni and prayed to propagate the Middle Way path. In the *King Giving of Instructions Sutra*,[12] Buddha prophesied:

> Ananda, this one who has generated bodhichitta
> And offered me this crystal mala,
> Shall, in future degenerate times, at the border of Dri and Den,
> Found a monastery known as the Virtuous,
> And be known by the name of Losang.
> He shall gather those of the four ordinations around him
> And will teach like Buddha in the sutras.
> In the temple with the leaf-enwreathed pillar,[13]
> He shall honor me and offer jeweled crowns to two likenesses of me.
> Through his making excellent prayers,
> His Teachings will endure for a thousand years.
> When he passes away from here,
> In a world to the northeast, Beautifully Arrayed with Wonder,
> He shall become the Buddha Lion's Roar.
> Those with faith in him shall be reborn there
> And that supreme realm shall be especially exalted!

With this, Buddha prophesied that Je Tsongkhapa would found the Virtuous, the Geden or Gelug tradition's Ganden Monastery between the regions of Drikung and Kyishö Den, that he would convene the Great Prayer Festival and offer golden crowns to the Jowo Shakyamuni and Jowo Akshobya Vajra statues of Buddha at the Lhasa Trulnang Cathedral, and that the fervent prayers he would make for the flourishing of Buddhadharma would extend the life of the Teachings in the world for a thousand years.

During Nagarjuna's lifetime, Kyabje Zong Rinpoche was Suryakirti, Chandrakirti's assistant at Nalanda. Chandrakirti, the elucidator of Buddha's wisdom teachings, was famous for terrifying and setting to flight an invading Dhuruka army by bringing a stone lion to life. Once, when entrusted with the monastery's livestock, he refused to take milk from the calves, and instead used his powers of samadhi to milk the *picture* of a cow! When the cows were left grazing outside, yet the supply of milk continued unabated, it was Suryakirti who had to explain the situation to the assembly. He must have been successful, because they took it in good humor, rather than expelling Chandrakirti for breaking the monastic rule of not revealing siddhis.

That was as much as I knew about Suryakirti until I took a break from writing this introduction to edit a translation that I had been working on for several years: *Lion of Siddhas: The Life and Teachings of Padampa Sangye.*[14] It includes an authoritative biography of Padampa Sangye by Chökyi Senge, the fourth incarnation of Jamyang Sheba, who was the author of Drepung Gomang Monastery's textbooks. I had not reviewed the details of Padampa Sangye's birth for some time. When I did I realized that Suryakirti was Chandrakirti's elder brother, and none other than the Indian acharya who would later become renowned to Tibetans as Padampa Sangye. I believe the evidence is clear and definitive; still, I want to emphasize that I take full responsibility for making this identification. Kyabje Zong Rinpoche has made no such claim.[15] In any case, Padampa Sangye was one of the most influential mahasiddhas of our millennium. His legendary life is said to have spanned 572 years (about 495-1067).[16] During that time he trained with legions of gurus, translated the six volumes of Mahasanghika Vinaya scriptures, became disillusioned with the monastic environment, practiced austerities at countless sites, traveled over twothirds of the earth, turned the wheel of Dharma three times in Tibet as a tantric mahasiddha, also came to Tibet as Kamalashila, the learned abbot who composed the *Stages of Meditation* treatises, and went to China to give the "swift enlightenment" teachings seminal to the development of the Chan and Zen schools. Some even identify Padampa Sangye with Bodhidharma.[17]

Padampa Sangye is particularly significant in the present context because he was instrumental in the development of Chöd in Tibet. He was Machig Labdrön's guru for Chöd, and assisted her in receiving recognition from the Indian pandits who had come to Tibet to examine her. Using his power of fleetfootedness, he headed an official investigation to check Machig Labdrön's claim that the body of her previous incarnation could be found at a particular site in India. In this way he helped the Chöd system formulated by Machig Labdrön become fully recognized and established.

After giving a description of his birthplace, his parents' occupations, and other details, Padampa Sangye's biography states that his parents had

> ... an eldest son, Ratnakirti; a middle son, Suryakirti; a younger son, Chandrakirti; and a sister, Padmakirti. Dampa was the middle son, Suryakirti.... His mother miraculously conceived without male contact during a time when his father was at sea. Afraid her husband would be angry, she swallowed poison and tried everything she could to abort the fetus, but was unable to destroy the vajra body. At that time she dreamt that many women were prostrating to her and circumambulating her. In the dream, as she elevated in space in meditation posture, a right-spiraling conch sounded, the sun soared as her cushion, the moon clothed her, and she traveled to the four continents. Riding a lion, she moved through the sky. The sun shone forth from her body, clearing the world's darkness. She saw innumerable portents of goodness and virtue, such as the building of ships and bridges for the liberation of multitudes of beings. At about three months into the pregnancy, the vowels and consonants of Sanskrit could be heard coming from her womb in four sessions throughout the day. At six months, recitation of the condensed *Perfection of Wisdom Sutra* and the *Expression of the Names of Manjushri* could be heard by anyone who came near, and all were astonished. His mother experienced many samadhis during that time. Then, with many wondrous omens such as light and music, without pain of childbirth, her baby was born. Immediately upon having been born, he asked, "Mother, are you well?" and, folding his palms together, recited praise of the Great Mother Prajnaparamita:

Beyond speech, thought, expression, wisdom gone beyond,
Unborn, unceasing, with a nature like space,
Discerning, transcendent wisdom's sphere of awareness,
Homage, O Mother of the three times' Buddhas!

Sages skilled in the reading of signs, upon examining him, said,
"The boy will follow in his father's vocation at first. Then, becoming a Buddhist monk, he will become a great pandit, master of the
five fields of knowledge. Then he will become a great lord of yogis,
a mahasiddha. His fame will spread in all directions like the sun."
Thus, in accordance with their prophecy, he was given the name
Suryakirti, which means "famed as the sun." When his father became
upset over his wife having had a child while he was at sea, Avalokiteshvara and Manjushri came in actuality, saying, "This son of yours
is a son of all the Buddhas! All sentient beings of this world are his
parents, not just you! His fortune is to be unconquerable!" Then his
father, the sea captain, believed in him and was delighted."[18]

Another of Kyabje Zong Rinpoche's previous incarnations was Lord
Atisha's lay disciple, Geshe Chagdri Chog. He was heir to Atisha's famous
precept, "Give up this life!" I remember Rinpoche answering a question
with the words: "For us, spiritual practice does not begin until we give up
this life!" Actual Dharma practice begins with mindfulness of death. Once
our intentions are influenced by awareness of the imminence of death,
this life's transitory pleasures and prestige will lose their luster. Without
that shift, Dharma cannot protect us from suffering, because our attention will gravitate back to those shortsighted goals.

The Yogi Chagdri Chog, who spent four years training with Atisha, is
said by Geshe Chen-nga-wa Lodrö Gyaltsen, Kyabje Phabongka Dechen
Nyingpo and others to have been a prior incarnation of Jetsun Milarepa.[19]
Again, Kyabje Zong Rinpoche has not made any claim to this effect, and
I am not trying to claim Milarepa for the Gelug. Of course, Je Tsongkhapa
and those of his lineage revere Milarepa highly. Je Tsongkhapa received
all of the teachings of Milarepa from the Kagyu Lama Chen-aga Rinpoche of the Pagdru Kagyu at Drikung, and the Ganden tradition con-

tinues to maintain unbroken transmission of Milarepa's life story, teachings and songs.

To me, many of Kyabje Zong Rinpoche's qualities mirrored those of Tibet's great yogi Milarepa, such as his industry in delighting the Guru with offering of practice and his perception of Dharma teachings in daily events and nature. We were always amazed, as well, by how Rinpoche's voice would flow along, "like a song," for hours, with quotations, logic, examples, and—especially—stories. His magical voice would enthrall listeners with the twists and turns of epic stories that transported them and left indelible imprints on their minds. Skilled in virtually all fields of knowledge, his vocal mastery was definitely striking. His Chöd initiations, for example, included call and response chanting between the guru and his disciples. It was hauntingly melodious, very inspiring, and uncommonly his own.

Anther previous incarnation of Kyabje Zong Rinpoche was Jetsun Galo (1203-1282) of the Galo Tulkus from Mi-nyak, Kham, in eastern Tibet. Jetsun Galo was an extraordinary being who took ordination at an early age, learned Sanskrit within three years, and became a master of Kalachakra with many disciples. He held the lineage of Vajra Bhairava Yamantaka, and mastered the Hevajra and Vajra Varahi tantras. He wrote many treatises on Tantric practice.

During the time of Je Tsongkhapa, Kyabje Zong Rinpoche's previous incarnation was Chöwang Dragpa of Shang-Shung (1404-1471).[20] He traveled to central Tibet and studied Sutra and Tantra extensively with Je Tsongkhapa and his successors, Gyaltsab Dharma Rinchen and Khedrub Geleg Pelsang. Recognized as an outstanding disciple by his gurus, he became the second throne holder of Jampa Ling Monastery in Chamdo, where he had many disciples. He established numerous monasteries, but his main seat was Trulda Namgyal Pelbarling in the Nakchu region of Kham, where he spent most of his life. He was well known for his writing and poetry on subjects such as the *Ramayana*, the life of Lotsawa Rinchen Zangpo, praises of Milarepa and Je Tsongkhapa, the Kalachakra initiation and commentary, the *Ornament of Clear Realizations*, grounds and paths, *lamrim*, and *lojong*. He was known for regularly attracting beggars to his room because he was always so kind to them, feeding and helping them.

Later, as "the Renunciant Lord of Siddhas," Jadral Drubwang Losang Namgyal (1670-1741), Rinpoche again played a pivotal role in upholding the Ganden tradition. He is remembered with gratitude for saving the transmission lineage of Panchen Losang Yeshe's teachings from being lost. Drubwang Losang Namgyal was renowned for his scriptural knowledge and realization of Tantra, and was the recognized holder of the Chakrasamvara and Mahamudra lineages. He practiced in solitary retreat near Reting Monastery, and later wandered widely, teaching in places such as Tsari, the sacred site of Heruka near the Indian border; Olka, the site of Je Tsongkhapa's austerities in the south; Dingri, where Padampa Sangye lived, in western Tibet; and Swayambhu Stupa in Nepal. He established his own monastic seat, Samdring, in Kyirong province, in southwestern Tibet. It was a principal center for Chöd practice, now re-established in Nepal. He taught at Gyutö Tantric College, specializing in the works of Atisha, Je Tsongkhapa and Panchen Losang Chökyi Gyaltsen. It is the Chöd commentary of Kyabje Zong Rinpoche's own prior incarnation as Drubwang Losang Namgyal that Rinpoche uses as the basis for the oral instructions that form the core of this book.[21] Rinpoche also draws heavily for the compilation of his Chöd Ganachakra on his predecessor's Chöd sadhana, the *Annihilation of Self-Grasping (Dagzin Tsarchöd)*, the most extensive Chöd practice in the Ganden tradition. It was Losang Namgyal's disciple, Tsechog Ling Kachen Yeshe Gyaltsen (1713-1793), who rose from humble beginnings to become the tutor of the Eighth Dalai Lama and the most prolific author and biographer of the Ganden Ear-Whispered Lineage.

TRANSCENDING PARTISANSHIP

Someone might think, "Impossible! Milarepa would never become a Gelugpa!" Or, "A Kagyu yogi could never take charge of a Gelugpa monastery!" Such thinking, clinging to supposedly irreconcilable differences between lineages, leans heavily toward sectarianism, which is something that Kyabje Zong Rinpoche, in full accord with Je Tsongkhapa, always warned against. He said that disparaging or discriminating against any lineage or facet of Buddha's teachings was equivalent to abandoning Dharma, the worst kind of nonvirtue imaginable, and quite contrary to Je Tsong-khapa's "Virtuous Tradition." In fact, one criticism that Tsongkhapa received from some who later became his greatest supporters was not that he was too *exclusive*, but that he was too *inclusive* and eclectic. For instance, he held fast to his conviction that Buddha's teachings were a union of Sutra and Tantra, even in the face of opposition from both sides, each of which wanted him to exclude the other. Seeking simply to rediscover Buddha's message for himself, Je Tsongkhapa transcended all sectarianism in his study and contemplation of the Teachings. With reverence, he sought out over fifty masters of all lineages of Buddhism in Tibet, discussing their instructions with them in their own debate courtyards, earning their respect, and very thoroughly researching the teachings in light of the Indian scriptures as well. He did not, however, simply build up an ency-clopedic knowledge of Dharma. Each time he reached his own conclu-sion as to what Buddha had intended, he put his understanding into practice as an instruction meant specifically for himself. This enabled him to compose, based on his own experience, crystal-clear roadmaps for Sutra and Tantra by which the entire path could be traversed with swiftness and ease. Devoting himself to his gurus and completing the path to enlight-enment, his pure example drew waves of disciples to him. It was his guru-devotion and his spiritual practice that brought him such universal success and respect. The verse of supplication used as Tsongkhapa's mantra is an example of this:

> Avalokiteshvara, treasure of unobjectified compassion,
> Manjushri, powerful lord of stainless wisdom,
> Je Tsongkhapa, crown jewel of Tibetan masters,
> At your feet, we beseech you.

It is a verse that Tsongkhapa originally offered in devotion to his great Sakya guru, Rendawa. The Venerable Rendawa then offered it back to him. This is the kind of mutual admiration and respect that characterizes the highest masters of all traditions.[22]

Like Je Tsongkhapa, Kyabje Zong Rinpoche transcended all bound-aries of lineage. In his characteristically direct way he once asked, "On what basis could I be partisan? My own family in this life and the families of my two previous incarnations were all Nyingma practitioners!" In another of his incarnations he was a Taglung Kagyu lama. Speaking personally, as a practitioner, I would seek only to inspire others with the knowledge that Kyabje Zong Rinpoche is a Buddha manifesting in our world. Buddhas need no defense from anyone, nor are they raised higher by anyone's praise, yet by developing faith in them we delight them and receive their blessings and inspiration. This, in turn, brings fulfillment of our true aspirations.

In regard to accomplishing the complete path to enlightenment, Kyabje Zong Rinpoche gave us this example: "If you want to get to the roof of a house that has ladders on all four sides, you must mount one of the ladders and climb it all the way to the top." Similarly, the four schools of Tibetan Buddhism all lead to complete enlightenment, but beginners must practice within one tradition if they wish to derive deep experience of it, and if they want to complete the path.

I count it as my greatest good fortune to have had the opportunity to practice Je Tsongkhapa's Ganden tradition long enough to have gotten even a glimpse of its many distinguished qualities. The Ganden tradition is a contribution of monumental proportions from the people of Tibet to the world, a tribute to all schools of Tibetan Buddhism. It is thanks to his Tibetan gurus of the Nyingma, Shijay,[23] Kadam, Kagyu, and Sakya traditions—along with direct guidance from Manjushri—that Je Tsongkhapa was able to attain his supreme realization, reinvigorating and extending the life of Buddhadharma in the world. As the Eighth Karmapa, Mikyö Dorje, said,

> When the Teachings of the Sakya, Kagyu, Kadam,
> And Nyingma sects in Tibet were declining,
> You, O Tsongkhapa, revived Buddha's Doctrine,
> Hence I sing this praise to you of Ganden Mountain.

And

> The trainees that walk in your footsteps
> Breathe the fresh air of the Great Way.

They would die for the good of the world!
Hence I sing this praise to you of Ganden Mountain.[24]

DIALECTICAL DEBATE AND THE MIDDLE WAY

Early in the biographical profile of Kyabje Zong Rinpoche that appears above, we see the central role that dialectical debate plays in the Ganden tradition's monastic training. Buddha himself said that his teachings should not be accepted out of mere respect but investigated through logical reasoning and one's own experience. One may quote the words of Buddha and other masters, but only one's own investigation and insight, one's own experience and practice, will bring about actual transformation. It was Lama Tsongkhapa's own investigative genius and insight that shaped his system's educational training, making it the vibrant, living form of Buddhism that it is today. Finding the tools of the ancient Indian logicians to be effective in illuminating every aspect of Sutra and Tantra, Je Tsongkhapa clarified—like Nagarjuna and Chandrakirti before him—the way in which logic can be used to unlock the secrets of Buddha's Middle Way path; that is, by using logical consequences to counter habitual ignorance's sense of reality.

Buddha used the metaphor of rubbing two sticks together until they catch fire and are consumed to describe a process by which conceptual analysis of the interdependent, conventional nature of existence can give rise to nonconceptual realization of selflessness that destroys belief in the independent reality of appearances. It is possible to misconstrue this to mean that realization of the ultimate somehow destroys conventional "reality," but this is not the case. Mere interdependent existence is in no way destroyed by emptiness or the wisdom realizing it, even though conventional appearances *do* disappear when emptiness is realized directly— that is, for anyone except a fully enlightened Buddha. Rather, it is ignorance's falsely imagined sense of an independent or truly existent self that is negated or "lost" in the realization of emptiness, and it is the ignorance that grasps that truly existent self that is undermined and destroyed. Only through meditation with appropriate motivation can such issues be investigated fully or have real impact upon the mind.

Discussion and dialectical debate, using precisely defined terms especially designed to describe inner experience, is another very valuable tool for the development of insight. After all, putting Dharma into words was considered to have been Buddha's supreme act of compassion. It was the only means by which Buddha could awaken beings from their trance of ignorance in order to induce them to cease creating and hallucinating their own suffering.

It is therefore critical to the welfare of living beings that no mistake is made when identifying the path of the Middle Way. It is characteristic of Lama Tsongkhapa's tradition to focus primary attention on any point that is essential or difficult, and the Middle Way Path, the very key to Buddha's compassionate liberation of beings, is profound and difficult to understand. During Tsongkhapa's time there were some in Tibet who thought the meaning of emptiness was nihilism, holding the Three Jewels and the law of karma to be completely baseless. Others, although they believed phenomena somehow existed, still claimed that all phenomena were neither existent *nor* nonexistent. Some made the claim that conventional phenomena only existed for consciousness that is totally mistaken; that they are not established by any sort of valid awareness. This had the disastrous effect of undermining conviction in the natural law of karmic cause and effect, the very foundation of spiritual practice. In fulfillment of the prophecy of Buddha Shakyamuni cited above, and the prayers made by the Brahmin youth when he offered Buddha the crystal mala, Je Tsongkhapa clarified the correct Middle Way view: phenomena do not exist from their own side, even down to the tiniest particle—but, at the same time, and because of that, karmic cause and effect function flawlessly. The glorious Protector Nagarjuna, whom Buddha himself prophesied would clarify the provisional and definitive meaning of the Teachings, said in his *Commentary on Bodhichitta,*

> This Teaching of karmic causality as compatible
> With knowledge of the emptiness of all phenomena!
> What could be more wonderful than this?
> What could be more unique than this?

When Buddha said that nonseeing is the highest or most sacred seeing, it was his supreme call to us to wake up and investigate whether the world actually exists in the way we perceive it. And it was his fearless proclamation that it does not that shakes us out of our complacency. Without this declaration from Buddha, it would be difficult for us to even *begin* to doubt our habitual way of perceiving things, much less realize that it is totally mistaken! That is why Buddha said we must hear Dharma from another, and why it is so profoundly meaningful to have encountered a guru who bears the lineage. No realized siddha has ever lacked a guru! When Buddha said, "The best seeing is nonseeing," he did not mean that we should just stop looking and investigating, or that language and thought are useless. If the Teachings are not contemplated, and cessation of thought is used as a principal method for meditation, the sticks of Buddha's metaphor will not be rubbed together, and no flame of insight will be ignited.

As Padampa Sangye said,

Kunga! It is incorrect to think that nothingness is the ultimate!

He also said,

Some meditate on nonconceptuality as the antidote to conceptual thought but you can't be liberated from samsara by doing that!

Asked, "Why is that?" Dampa answered,

Seeking nonconceptuality doesn't compare with realizing suchness! You understand the root meaning neither conceptually *nor* nonconceptually! In that case, Dharma doesn't become the antidote to delusion, so even if you know the three *pitaka*s, it won't help your mind![25]

The traditional view holds that, during a middle phase of Padampa Sangye's remarkable life, he came to Tibet in the late eighth century as the great abbot Kamalashila. Kamalashila was his ordination name, the one often recited in Padampa Sangye's name mantras. At that time, he was invited to Tibet to debate with the Chinese monk Hashang Mahayana, who was propounding a position that one should withdraw the mind from everything. Kamalashila won the debate, and cessation of thought was rejected as a principal means to enlightenment. Kamalashila composed extensive, middling, and brief treatises called the *Stages of Meditation (Gom Rim)*, which are still used as authoritative guides.

Once one has developed insight into interdependence, the conventional *becomes* the gateway to the ultimate. As one understands that "self" only exists as a label, "I," upon various physical and mental experiences that arise and subside in a constant state of flux, it becomes obvious that there is nothing to which that very thought "I" can refer that comes from anywhere, goes anywhere, or could be self-sustaining in the slightest. An understanding of this sort is what is referred to as the view of the Middle Way, a conceptual understanding of emptiness which, through meditation, is then deepened into actual vipashyana insight.

In Hinayana tenet systems, Buddha did not emphasize the explanation of the emptiness of phenomena other than that of a personal identity. From that perspective, a phrase such as "thought without a thinker," or "action without an agent" might be considered correct if the thinker or agent is considered as the person, and the thought or action is considered as the aggregate. But, as Chandrakirti points out, without giving up belief in the real existence of the aggregates, one cannot actually give up the "view of the transitory collection" that clings to the belief in a personal identity, either.

In Mahayana tenet systems, Buddha taught that thought has no more reality that the thinker, action no more reality than its agent. Each exists only relative to the other and not otherwise. From that standpoint, it makes practical sense that, of course, thought does not exist without a thinker, or action without an agent. By examining their interdependent natures, we can come to understand the emptiness of any independent self-nature. The realization that both subject and object are missing when their deepest mode of existence is seen directly gives rise to an inexpressible experience of nonduality.

Conventionally, phenomena *do* exist, interdependently, like reflections, while at the same time they are empty of independent or inherent existence from the ultimate point of view. If the perspective of a statement switches from conventional to ultimate in mid-course, without any distinction being made, someone trying to understand might conclude that the main point is to just stop thinking, because the words don't make any sense!

In the Ganden tradition, great emphasis is placed upon clarity of expression. During dialectical debate, in particular, effort is made to ascertain that contexts are not confused so that communication does not become garbled. Recognizing the limitations of language, as well as how it functions in connection with consciousness, the skilled debater uses language with compassion to coherently and seamlessly guide trainees to subtle conceptual and direct realizations, including the inexpressible realization of selflessness that leads to liberation and full enlightenment.

Kyabje Zong Rinpoche's mastery of the tool of dialectical debate was legendary. It is, of course, difficult to support *any* position expressed in words as perfect or correct, but Rinpoche could undermine even a skilled debater's position. In the biography we read of the reluctance of some older monks to face him in debate, afraid that they might lose face before the assembly. If debaters were always afraid to lose, even in daily debate practice, their pride would probably prevent them from learning. At the time of public debate, however, the social and emotional dynamic is especially heightened. A monk, his class and his monastery's respect are subject to intense public scrutiny. It would be hard to fault those elder monks for assessing their own knowledge and capabilities realistically, and saving themselves and their classmates some embarrassment. Ideally, however, dialectical debate takes spiritual aspirants into a deep and transformative examination of their own identities that enables them to give up a fixed sense of ego and become more flexible and skillful in handling all kinds of situations. Still, only the rare heroic being is completely confident and immune to public opinion. In his present incarnation, Kyabje Zong Rinpoche is demonstrating the same confident experience in dialectical debate that he exhibited in his previous life.

PUTTING STUDY TO USE IN PRACTICE

It is typical of the Ganden tradition that Kyabje Zong Rinpoche brings the scholarly language of the teachings on mind and cognition (*lorig*) into his discussion of emptiness meditation, emphasizing that study must be put to practical use. In the course of an oral instruction of this type, it is, of course, impossible to cover all of the background knowledge that would be assumed in many of his listeners. So here is a rough outline of the system's tenets pertinent to the discussion.

All existent phenomena, from forms to omniscience, have a conventional nature and an ultimate nature. Both of these natures exist because they can be realized. The ultimate nature is a negative phenomenon, meaning that it is realized through the explicit negation of something. It is an absence that can be realized, a sacred liberating truth, the ultimate mode of existence of all that exists. That which is negated in realization of emptiness is not something that actually exists, but a mode of existence of which thought falsely conceives. It is therefore, very useful to understand how thought operates.

Except for yogic direct perception or moments of clairvoyance, and our sense consciousnesses, most of our perceptible mental activity consists of thought, so we may as well make the best of it—at least until we have a better option. Unlike direct perception, thought realizes its object by way of a generic image. These generic images form as one learns to speak. When a child first hears the word "tree," and sees a pine tree, for example, it starts to associate the sound "tree" with that remembered image. The next time it hears the word—in reference to, perhaps, a poplar or bonsai—that image will be revised. Gradually it takes on the "generic image" of a tree, which is nothing more than the exclusion of everything that is not a tree. It functions to associate trees with the word "tree," and to understand and talk about trees. That is how conceptual thought works; it apprehends a word and a meaning as suitable to be mixed. In general, things can be known either through direct perception, or through thought. Direct perception is rich with actual perception of its object and is much more powerful than conceptual thought. Thought is impoverished, in that it understands its object only through a mental image, and it is mistaken, in that its object, a sort of isolated class, appears to be the object itself.

Yet even though conceptual thought lacks the power of direct perception, it is indispensable for discovering certain things that are hidden from direct perception at first. For instance, samsaric beings are not able to real-ize that their own mental continuums have never been separate from their ultimate natures, and so those beings remain bound in suffering. By engag-ing in ultimate analysis, one can develop insight that contradicts ignorance's erroneous perception of self and can realize its actual mode of existence. Knowledge of the nature of generic images makes it possible to under-stand how ignorance could conceive of something that doesn't exist. And once that "object of negation" is stably recognized, the target for the arrow of emptiness meditation has been identified. In the next moment, one is set to realize its absence. At first, one's understanding of emptiness depends more on the words, a "sound generality." As understanding devel-ops further, the conceptual image becomes clearer and subtler. The sense of an objective emptiness and a subjective viewer fade by turns until the generic image dissolves completely and emptiness is realized directly. It is as if the actual object is something so subtle that it cannot not be seen unless we keep looking steadily in the same direction.

When Rinpoche explains how to meditate on emptiness at the conclu-sion of the sadhana, he instructs us to visualize that all appearances, gods and ghosts, melt into light and dissolve into our hearts. Then, with the spacelike appearance that arises, he tells us to feel that we are seeing empti-ness. This is the appearing object. Then, to focus on the actual understand-ing of emptiness, we think, "this appearance of emptiness does not exist from its own side." That which is ascertained or understood is the con-ceived object.[26] Analyzing with the logic of interdependent origination, we conclude that none of the "three spheres"—agent, action, or object—exist from their own sides. Once analysis is complete, we cease it, and set-tle in the spacelike experience of emptiness that follows. Without labeling or objectifying it at all, we remain absorbed for as long as possible. On arising, the practice is continued; all appearances are seen as dreamlike illu-sions arising from emptiness, like waves rising and falling in the ocean.

From the Tantric point of view, this meditation remains conceptual until the inner energy winds dissolve into the central channel at the heart chakra, and the knots constricting the channel there are loosened. At that point, actual clear light is experienced, and illusory body, union, and full enlightenment will soon follow. Je Tsongkhapa, in his commentary on

Chöd, says that we should practice this meditation on emptiness at that
level, if we can.

MAINTAINING PURE VIEW OF THE GURU

Kyabje Zong Rinpoche speaks about the kinds of deeds of which siddhas
are capable, such as healing, affecting the weather, living over a thousand
years, levitation, flight, speed-walking, passing through the earth, far-sightedness, invisibility, and so forth. He also tells of Kyabje Phabongka
Dechen Nyingpo's previous life as the mahasiddha Krishnapada,[27] and
other stories involving the inconceivable deeds of other lineage gurus. He
makes the point that since it is easy to misinterpret a guru's deeds when
he or she displays realized tantric conduct, we must make prayers always
to be able to see that the guru is Buddha.

Often, great tantric mahasiddhas were not able to remain in Buddhist
monasteries because their actions were incomprehensible to the general
sangha or appeared to transgress the vows. At a certain point on the path
of Buddhist Tantra, the disciple is authorized by the Vajra Master to perform miraculous deeds more openly for the benefit of beings as a means
to perfecting the accumulations necessary for enlightenment. It is a highly
advanced stage at which the disciple is practically certain to attain enlightenment in his or her lifetime. The Tibetan term for tantric conduct, *tül-
shug chöpa*, has been translated variously as "vanquishing conduct," "crazy
wisdom conduct," and so on. Literally, the term means the lifestyle conduct of "subduing and entering." The practitioner has "subdued" the hal-
lucinations of ignorance and "entered" the divine world of the Guru
Yidam. At the generation stage of Highest Yoga Tantra, this occurs
through imagination and meditative stabilization. For this type of tantric
conduct, however, completion stage realization is required. The energies
that flow through the side channels of the subtle body that support
deluded minds have also been "subdued," and have "entered" into the central channel. At this point, all phenomena are actually experienced as the
nondual bliss-void nature of the Deity. The practitioner experiences everything as of a single divine taste and sees the Guru Yidam in *all* phenomena, pure and deluded, clean and filthy, alike. The yogi's actions will not

conform to common opinion and may very well appear crazy to others, so they sometimes may have to leave the boundaries of organized religion. They just continue benefiting beings in the inconceivable dance of full enlightenment.

We may not be able to understand a guru's deeds, but once we have become the disciple of a qualified guru, we must take care to maintain a pure view of him or her. In the Ganden tradition, the following prayer is recited:

> May I never develop, for even an instant,
> Mistaken views of my glorious Gurus' deeds!
> Through devotion, seeing all they do as excellent,
> May the Gurus' blessings enter my mind!

Padampa Sangye took refuge in his gurus with the lines:

> I prostrate and go for refuge to the holy Gurus!
> Please bless me to fully awaken soon!
> Until full awakening, as well, please bless me to have
> Inconceivable awe and devotion for the holy Gurus!

Kyabje Zong Rinpoche's immutable pure devotion to his Gurus, His Holiness the fourteenth Dalai Lama, Kyabje Phabongka Dechen Nyingpo, and Kyabje Trijang Dorje Chang, is fully evident in the material presented here. He had an especially close connection with Kyabje Trijang Dorje Chang (1901-1981). He sometimes said that Kyabje Trijang Dorje Chang was the "director of us all." And no wonder, for Kyabje Trijang Dorje Chang was of the Buddha Amitabha incarnation lineage of Geshe Langri Tangpa, Khedrub Je, Gyalwa Ensapa, Panchen Losang Chökyi Gyaltsen, and Panchen Losang Yeshe![28] He was the guru of practically every Gelugpa lama of his generation. I pray that all beings on earth continue to merit the enlightened leadership of such great beings!

PRACTICING WITH THE WISDOM OF COMPASSION

The three principal paths—renunciation, bodhichitta, and wisdom realizing emptiness—are what distinguish Buddhist Tantra from other systems. They are the most succinct form of *lamrim* and *lojong,* those precious gifts Lord Atisha bequeathed to all the people of Tibet. The instruction called *The Three Principal Paths* is an important Ganden oral lineage transmission that Je Tsongkhapa received directly from Manjushri. Kyabje Zong Rinpoche emphasizes the three principal paths throughout the commentary as that which really empowers the practice, and he shows how all three involve giving up inherently existent self. Investigating the Four Noble Truths with intelligence by realizing that suffering is caused by ignorance, and that wisdom realizing selflessness can act as its antidote, a practitioner of sharp faculties establishes the validity of the enlightening path, and enters it joyfully, with full confidence that it can be accomplished. Those of sharp faculties can also make best use of *lojong,* mind training, to develop uniquely powerful and irreversible bodhichitta. As Bodhisattva Shantideva said, "If one is unable to trade one's own happiness for others' suffering, there can be no enlightenment, nor any happiness in the world!" Rinpoche makes it clear that the compassionate determination to free all beings from suffering through one's own enlightenment, the good heart of bodhichitta, is most precious of all. The methods to take negative circumstances onto the path and *tonglen* meditation, in particular, are unequalled sources of inner strength and joy. Chöd is the most dynamic and profound enactment of these.

Chöd practitioners, with the awareness of death and the dreamlike nature of existence, seek to return the inconceivable kindness of all mother beings and embark on the path, never looking back. Realizing that the wasteland of their previous incarnations is like a vast charnel ground, they take delight in being able to sacrifice themselves, this once at least, for the sake of the Dharma and the welfare of beings. Unable to bear the needless torment of beings, practitioners face death head on, transforming it into the spiritual path. They reemerge with the healing medicine of the Great Mother, bringing harmony to all beings and the environment.

We are indebted to Tenzin Paksam for the original translation of the oral instructions, and to Geshe Losang Tsultrim for the biographical profile, research assistance, and additional translations. I edited and annotated both parts, and made the translations included in the appendices. I must therefore take full responsibility for any errors. I pray that Kyabje Zong Rinpoche's instructions may once again help to promote and facilitate the practice of Chöd in the Ganden tradition.

In the final two appendices, I offer translations of Gungthang Tenpai Dronme's prayer for the flourishing of the Ganden tradition, and His Holiness the Dalai Lama's prayer for the flourishing of *all* of the wonderful traditions of Tibetan Buddhism.[29]

David Molk
Ganden Samten Ling
Morning Glory Ranch
Big Sur, California
May 27, 2005

Chöd in the Ganden Tradition:

The Oral Instructions

Lineage thangka for Ganden Chöd tradition

ᑌᑎ An Overview of the Practice of Chöd

CHÖD IS THE ESSENCE of Prajnaparamita.[30] It focuses on attaining bodhichitta[31] and realizing emptiness. These are the central practices of Buddhism. There are many ways of generating bodhichitta, such as the instructions on Sevenfold Cause and Effect, or the Equalizing and Exchange of Self with Others. Chöd deals with severing self-cherishing mind and with cherishing others more than oneself. The Tibetan word *chöd* means "cutting."

Self-grasping mind is the root of samsaric existence. In order to cut this root, wisdom understanding emptiness is required. For these reasons, Chöd teaches wisdom of emptiness and the method of attaining bodhichitta.

In general, Mahayana paths have two aspects: bodhichitta, and wisdom realizing emptiness. Chöd purifies negativity and gathers the accumulations necessary for the attainment of these two through offering of the body as nectar to the enlightened beings, offering of the body to spirits, and meditation on emptiness.

LINEAGE OF THE PRACTICE

There is much scriptural reference for Chöd practice. For example, in a previous life, Buddha Shakyamuni was a bodhisattva who offered his body to a starving tigress. There are also stories of other bodhisattvas who offered their bodies to other sentient beings.

There are both close and distant lineages for this Chöd teaching. The distant lineage has two divisions: of vastness and of profundity. The distant lineage of vastness begins with Buddha Shakyamuni, goes through

Maitreya, Asanga, and Vasubandhu, and eventually comes to Je Tsong-khapa.[32] The distant lineage of profundity begins with Buddha Shakya-muni, goes through Manjushri, Nagarjuna, and Aryadeva, and again comes to Je Tsongkhapa.

The close lineage of this Chöd teaching begins with Buddha Vajrad-hara, goes through Manjushri, and then goes directly to Pawo Dorje and Je Tsongkhapa. Je Tsongkhapa practiced Chöd extensively. Eventually this lineage came to the first Panchen Lama. [At present, it is held by Kyabje Zong Rinpoche.]

Practitioners of this close lineage include Gyalwa Ensapa and Dhar-mavajra. Dharmavajra is, in fact, still alive, but ordinary beings are unable to perceive him. This lineage includes the closest disciples of Je Tsong-khapa. Three, known as the "vajra brothers,"[33] are still alive in Tibet near Lhasa, Talaypa, and Panam. Some fortunate beings have had visions of these practitioners. For example, there was a Sera monk who was doing a fire puja on a mountain near Lhasa when he saw a large monastery with many practitioners. They spoke to him and asked him to remain with them, but he left in order to sell his property at Sera. When he tried to return to the monastery, he could not; it was gone. In actuality, there are still many hidden valleys in Tibet. The Chinese will never find these.

One of these "vajra brother" disciples of Je Tsongkhapa, Sangye Yeshe, was given a special text by a dakini. This text was from Guru Rinpoche. Sangye Yeshe gave the text to the third Dalai Lama.

In the hills and mountains of Tibet, many shepherds hear the sounds of rituals but never see the adepts conducting those rituals. Pawo Dorje was one such shepherd who heard Manjushri's mantra spontaneously. He developed great bliss upon hearing these holy sounds and eventually had close direct contact with Manjushri. When Je Tsongkhapa was young, he needed Pawo Dorje as an intermediary and interpreter for Manjushri. Later on, he received visions of Manjushri, and was directly cared for by Man-jushri. There are many biographies of Je Tsongkhapa, an example of which is a detailed one recently obtained from Mongolia by Guru Deva.

Dharmavajra is still alive and lives on Mount Panam in Tibet. This mountain is the actual mandala palace of Guhyasamaja. On the eastern side of Mount Panam there is a cave with a waterfall in it. Usually this water, once it has hit the ground, disappears if it is touched. At certain times, however, if the water falls on someone's head and then onto the ground, it will transform into sacred relics. The cave, called Pemasemuche, is a pilgrimage site in Tsang province.

Mount Panam itself is not very large, and is surrounded by other mountains. Guru Rinpoche and others tied these flying mountains down with stakes. In the area are two small towns with a nunnery and a monastery. It is a place made famous by Nangsa, a Tibetan woman who "died" and came back to life. The great monastery of Tashilhunpo, established by the first Dalai Lama, is about two days' journey from Mount Panam. From this monastery, monks set out to collect the water from Pemasemuche Cave and then distribute it as the blessings of Dharmavajra. On the full moon of the fourth Tibetan month, the waterfall transforms into milky water that is regarded as the bodhichitta of practitioners.

Also near Mount Panam is Ensa Monastery. About seventy-five of Gyalwa Ensapa's monks used to live at this monastery. They were distinctive in being permitted to wear pandits' hats in debates and pujas. This is a very important and precious place. Gyalwa Ensapa's body was kept there. When he died, his body became very small, a cubit in height, while his head remained the same size. It is a difficult journey on horseback to reach this monastery.

When Gyalwa Ensapa was about five or six years old, he did not have many clothes, and had to wrap himself in blue cloth. Even at that age he won a debate with a Sakya geshe. The geshe was astonished, and thought that he was a spirit. The geshe was even more surprised when Gyalwa Ensapa recited some of the *Eight Thousand Verse Perfection of Wisdom Sutra* to him in Sanskrit. The geshe then washed his bowl and offered tea to Gyalwa Ensapa, showing him deep reverence.

Once, when Gyalwa Ensapa had contracted smallpox, he happened to hear Dharmavajra reciting Je Rinpoche's *Praise of Dependent Arising*. Due to the intense faith he felt upon hearing it, he rapidly recovered, and sought teachings from Dharmavajra at Ensa Monastery. Eventually, Gyalwa Ensapa gained enlightenment in his lifetime.

Gyalwa Ensapa's closest disciple was Khedrub Sangye Yeshe, next of the close lineage gurus of Chöd. Sangye Yeshe did not reincarnate; he was reabsorbed by the emanator. Gyalwa Ensapa's incarnation, however, came to be recognized as the first Panchen Lama, who had his monastic seat at Tashilhunpo. The first Panchen Lama, Losang Chökyi Gyaltsen, should therefore actually be regarded as the "second" Panchen Lama, Gyalwa Ensapa being the first.[34] Panchen Losang Chökyi Gyaltsen composed the Chöd practice called *Guide for Those Seeking Liberation*.[35]

Panchen Losang Chökyi Gyaltsen's Chöd teachings were eventually passed to the tutor of the eighth Dalai Lama, Kachen Yeshe Gyaltsen,[36] who wrote commentaries on the practice. We will be using a text written by Losang Namgyal,[37] and referring to commentaries composed by Kachen Yeshe Gyaltsen.[38]

The close lineage passed to Kyabje Phabongka[39] from Mochog Rinpoche, who had visions of Avalokiteshvara. Kyabje Zong Rinpoche also received these Chöd teachings from Mochog Rinpoche.

The main monastery associated with this lineage of Chöd practice is Samdring, originally in Kyirong province, now re-established in Nepal. This monastery is famed for its authentic rituals. They are pure because the founder of the monastery, Losang Namgyal, was a highly realized being.

Finally, when discussing the lineage of the Chöd system, mention must be made of Machig Labkyi Drölma, also known as Machig Labdrön.[40] She was an emanation of Great Mother Prajnaparamita, Dakini Sukhasiddhi, and Tara. This female enlightened being was a very extraordinary woman. In her previous life she was an Indian yogi. He was encouraged by his yidam to go to Tibet but did not go immediately, spending periods of time in retreat at Bodh Gaya. He passed away without going to Tibet and, in his next life, was born as Machig Labkyi Drölma in Tibet. *Machig* means "Great Mother," *Lab* was her family name, and *Drölma* means "Tara."

Machig Labkyi Drölma promoted Chöd extensively during her lifetime, and wrote a volume on the practice to answer questions of her disciples.[41] She had several children, including a son born while she was traveling in Tibet, who became a great practitioner.[42]

Some of the melodies used in this Chöd system are those composed by Machig Labdrön herself, particularly the section on the body being cut up. This melody was inspired by the sound of flapping wings of vultures arriving for a "sky-burial." There are two versions of the melody, a long and a short one. It is important to remember that the Chöd melodies are not the compositions of chanting beggars, but the wisdom of Buddha in actuality. For that reason, reciting Chöd authentically, to the original melodies, creates great merit. In the same way, *Guru Puja* must be kept pure. If the melodies degenerate, the authenticity and blessings will be lost.[43]

This system of Chöd is explained in three main parts: place of practice, basis of practice, and advice on practice, including the results of practice.

PLACE OF PRACTICE

In order to practice Chöd, we should go to a cemetery, or wherever there are spirits. The best place is the more frightful. Why is this? It is easier to practice in a graveyard because identifying the self-grasping mind that clings to an independent self is accomplished more quickly and easily in a terrifying place. That is why such places are chosen. However, we should seek fearful places only in accordance with our experience and bravery. As our strength of mind develops, we should definitely seek more terrifying places such as graveyards and mountaintops, but to begin with, we should practice in our rooms until we are accustomed to the sadhana, and then we can begin to practice without a candle. Also, a good place to begin is anywhere that has been blessed by earlier great teachers. Only when a practitioner is highly realized should he or she go alone to cemeteries.

This particular text[44] does not mention specific qualities of the place. Other commentaries give extensive explanations of suitable places, as well as accounts of the previous lives of Machig Labkyi Drölma in India. Such commentaries have many questions and answers for advanced practitioners, but are difficult for beginners.

Why is this practice done alone and usually at night? In order to sever self-grasping, we purposely rouse it through fear, and then destroy it through bodhichitta and the realization of emptiness. When fear arises we must thoroughly search for the self that is threatened and, at the same time, let go of the body that is threatened. Fear of such appearances to mind can be extinguished by generating bodhichitta coupled with the realization that we can now give our body to the spirits, who have all been our kind mothers in previous lifetimes. We can thereby also make the connection in order to teach them Dharma in the future. Thus, a pure dedication for this practice would be as follows:

> As this is my best chance to repay their kindness,
> May all these spirits be satisfied with my body!
> By giving my body, may all faults of samsara be purified, as well!
> May all obstacles to Dharma practitioners be overcome!
> And may all great teachers live long, until the end of samsara!

So we can see that the aim of practicing alone and at night is a very precious and meaningful one.

Initially, we should practice Chöd alone in our rooms at night, quietly, with less fear. It is by gradually developing bodhichitta and wisdom realizing emptiness—not by just becoming braver—that we can confidently realize that whatever appears or happens can be transformed into the path. At that point, we should become more determined in our place of practice. Do not, under any circumstances, endanger your life in the choice of place. Unless we have great experience, we should never do this practice in any place that is threatened by falling rocks or trees, possible floods, or the threat of a collapsing house. Eventually, when we achieve full confidence in Chöd, there is no need to go to violent places at all. This is because terrifying visions will appear wherever we are. That is important because we need terrifying visions of spirits if we are to practice Chöd sincerely.

People have different mental capacities for fear. Some are too brave, some are too afraid. Both of these types of people will find Chöd difficult. We must have *some* fear for this practice to be successful. A desperate search for the "I" causes fear to develop. The best method for overcoming this fear is bodhichitta and wisdom realizing emptiness. It is because of the need for fear that practice should be done alone. Any group retreat on Chöd lessens the fear involved. Engaging in the practice at night also increases the necessary fear.

If we are going to practice in cemeteries or places like that, we must avoid unnecessary fear. Carefully examine the place in daylight so as to distinguish what is there. One graveyard in Tibet had a reliquary house for *tsa-tsa* statues[45] that was surrounded by nettles. A Chöd practitioner did not examine this cemetery beforehand, so when he experienced fear during his practice, he mistook the reliquary house for a spirit, and the nettles and branches for the spirit's arms. As a result, when he fell into the nettles and felt his robe caught by the branches, he experienced such fear that he ran away, leaving his damaru next to the reliquary house!

We should not be *too* afraid. We must train the mind carefully. Whatever appears to us, our minds should remain calm. We may see images and hear sounds. Developing fear, our hair may stand up and we may want to flee. But it is precisely at this moment of fear that we should search carefully for the "I" that is afraid. We should then give up this "I" by offering our bodies to our fears, and mixing our minds with space. In this way we will find that the "I" does not exist, and we will realize emptiness.

It is difficult to identify the object negated in emptiness if we only do this practice in our rooms, however. We need to go to frightful places to clarify the "I" that is to be negated. It is through examining our fears that we attain precious results. If our minds are mixed with space, and our bodies have been offered to spirits, then where is a concrete, independent "I," or self? It seems that it must be there with the body or the mind, yet both of these no longer exist in the way they did before. Realizing spacelike emptiness, all our fears will be pacified.

The purpose of doing Chöd practice in frightful places is not only to realize emptiness, but also to develop bodhichitta. Having offered our body to the spirits, there is no longer any need to care about it. We should really visualize our blood as an ocean for the spirits to drink, our body as food for the spirits to eat. It is for the sake of all mother sentient beings that we give up our bodies. "Exchanging self for others" in a graveyard is a very powerful method for developing bodhichitta, because all attachment to the body ceases.

Without fear, Chöd cannot be practiced. It is fear for the "I" that causes the desperate search for an "I" to hold on to. When the nonexistence of an inherently existent, independent "I" is directly perceived, then we are realizing emptiness. The antidote to such fear is bodhichitta motivation.

This is very significant. The place of Chöd practice amplifies the necessary fear.

BASIS FOR PRACTICE

"Basis for the practice of Chöd," in this context, refers to the motivation of the practitioner. A Chöd practitioner must have two motivations. He or she must be disillusioned with the attractions of samsara. Just as a banana tree, if skinned, reveals no core or essence, samsara must also be seen as essenceless. Even long-lived gods suffer rebirth. All samsaric wealth can turn to poverty. Impermanence, alone, is certain.

In addition, the Chöd practitioner must have bodhichitta, seeking enlightenment in order to benefit others. Whenever Chöd is practiced, these two motivations must be present, because, without proper motivation, beneficial results will not be attained. Instead, harm will result. Some people practice Chöd out of a motive to seek fame and offerings, or out of jealousy and competitiveness. The results of such incorrect motivation for the sake of this life's concerns are decrease of the practitioner's faith, increase of hindrances and illness, and the inability to be with spiritual friends.

In general, even if we practice the other perfections, if we do not practice pure moral conduct, we will not gain another precious human rebirth. Only very few beings practice pure moral conduct. Only very few beings uphold their tantric vows. The pratimoksha vows are, themselves, very difficult to keep. The consequence of this is that very few will regain the precious human rebirth. We can thus see that it is essential to begin now to try to insure a fortunate rebirth for the next life.

We must take refuge in the Three Jewels with unshakable faith. However, this faith alone will not liberate us from samsara. Always remember that even human beings are never free from the sufferings of birth, death, old age, sickness, hunger, and all types of mental sufferings. Beggars and monks have the least suffering; people with many children tend to have greater suffering than solitary people. The pleasures of this life become causes that lure us into more suffering. Dharma practitioners forget the practice of Dharma when involved in pleasures. Therefore, for us now, the most important practice is pure renunciation. It is only through this that we can liberate others still caught in samsara. The practices of a bodhisattva are impossible without the renunciation of self-interest and the cherishing of others. In order to renounce self-interest, we must identify and renounce a truly existent self.

Je Tsongkhapa emphasized that there are three principal paths: renunciation, bodhichitta, and wisdom. Without renunciation, no other practice will be very useful for future lives. If we have no motivation to free ourselves, then what is the use of other practices purporting to help free others? Once we generate renunciation purely, we must also develop bodhichitta from the very beginning. If we do not, or if we fail to maintain it, we will fall to the Hinayana path of primarily seeking our own liberation. Even so, if a Mahayanist were to fall to lower realms, he or she would still be in a better position than Hinayana Arhats enjoying the solitary bliss of peace. Due to the development of precious bodhichitta mind, once liberated from that hell, the bodhisattva's way to full enlightenment would be swift, whereas it might be eons before the Hinayana Arhats could be awakened from their solitary peace and continue on their way to full enlightenment. And—whatever our motivation, whether Mahayanist or Hinayanist—if we do not realize emptiness-wisdom, we will not gain liberation in any vehicle. We must attain the pure correct view of the nontrue existence of self.

Renouncing this life and samsaric rebirth is, indeed, pure renunciation, but renunciation does not stop there. We must also give up the true existence of self for the attainment of bodhichitta and wisdom. Relative bodhichitta *gives up* self in the aspiration to liberate other beings, whereas ultimate bodhichitta *understands* the nontrue existence of self.[46] All of these three principal paths are therefore forms of renunciation, and are based in pure renunciation of samsara that arises from close familiarity with impermanence and suffering.

Practice of Chöd spurs us to develop bodhichitta and realize emptiness. An essential preliminary for Chöd practice is pure renunciation; otherwise, we will have no firm foundation on which to build. Likewise, without pure bodhichitta, we will not be able to practice the generation and completion stages of Highest Yoga Tantra. Chöd practice is the best skillful means to eliminate obstacles and hindrances to the development of pure bodhichitta.

If we have not developed bodhichitta, Chöd practice will be good only for begging tsampa. It has been prophesied that during this degenerate age there will be such practitioners. They will wear strange clothes and have long malas. They will carry whips to defend themselves from dogs.

What are the characteristics of a pure Chöd practitioner? Such a person first needs empowerment and the oral transmission of the teachings. Stable practice of renunciation and bodhichitta are necessary. Just wandering around with a thighbone and damaru is no good to anyone. We should have no grasping for wealth or possessions; they have no meaning. We should view our bodies in the same way. Do not grasp at them. Upon examination, nothing of use to future lives can be found amongst our possessions, or connected with our bodies.

We need not give up all wealth and possessions; we can just stop clinging to them and, instead, use our wealth skillfully for practice. If we have attachment when we die, even to just one object, this will greatly hinder our consciousness. How many things are we attached to at this very moment? It is very important, above all, to have no attachment to our bodies.

It is by seeing the essencelessness of samsara that we develop the minds of loving-kindness and compassion for sentient beings who suffer due to their delusions about the nature of samsara. When these joyful minds arise, we must act as their willing servants. Usually we work very hard as slaves to the three poisons. These joyful minds free us from such bondage.

Practice of Dharma is like a mirror. It is only by using a mirror that we can see the dirt on our faces. We must use the mirror of practice to assess ourselves, to look inward, searching for our own faults. Usually we do not see our own faults, only those of others. Through the practice of Dharma, we can perceive our own faults and correct them.

Once we become honest about our own faults and perceive the essenceless nature of samsara, we can become empowered with loving-kindness and compassion. When this happens we will be able to uproot the apprehension of the true existence of ourselves and other phenomena. The practice of Chöd is a way to destroy these powerful delusions, but it must be founded upon this special "empowerment" of joyful mind.

Before one engages in the practice of Chöd, it is essential to engage in these preliminary meditations on renunciation and bodhichitta. Because these are meditations cultivated "within" ourselves, they are termed the mind-training of "internal cutting." If we do not yet have pure renunciation or bodhichitta, but have pure motivation and the wish to develop these holy minds, Chöd practice can be very helpful. However, if we do not have pure motivation, neither clothes nor ritual objects will help. If we engage in Chöd practice with impure motivation, and try to subdue spirits in order to harm others, pure yogis will suffer criticism, and we will receive much hindrance and illness, losing all respect and help of others. The preliminary meditations on "internal cutting" are therefore extremely important.

It is also vital to take refuge purely and correctly prior to engaging in the practice of Chöd. Before every session, remember how difficult it is to obtain a precious human rebirth. Such a rebirth is precious both temporarily and ultimately. Thinking along these lines, strongly determine to make full use of this life. Otherwise, life is like a man without heart; it has no true purpose or meaning. We should realize that we have gained all the external and internal circumstances conducive for the practice of Dharma, and that we must practice in this very lifetime, from this very moment. Yet we are pushed by karmic impulses *not* to want to create the causes of happiness, be it the temporary well-being of high rebirth, or the ultimate happiness of liberation and enlightenment. That is why we must recollect the sufferings of lower realms. By contemplating our karmic formations, we can see that it is as if we had swallowed a great deal of poison. We must become determined to take no more poison in the future. Seeking help and guidance, we generate unshakable faith in the Three Jewels as the only objects of refuge.

Whenever taking refuge, it is very beneficial to bring to mind the qualities of the Three Jewels. It is by understanding the qualities of Buddha that we can realize the qualities of Dharma and can attain the qualities of Sangha. For example, Buddha's speech has sixty qualities that can liberate many sentient beings simultaneously, teaching each according to his or her capacity to understand. Nothing is unknown to the omniscient mind of Lord Buddha. Buddha's loving-kindness is vast, with more than motherly love for all living creatures, being impartial, skillful, and able to actually help in this life and all others. It is only we who hinder, who obstruct Buddha's power through lack of faith. Buddha was once an ordinary being like us who attained all these wonderful qualities through the practice of Dharma. Thinking in this way, we can realize the power of Dharma. The Sangha are those who correctly understand Dharma, keep their vows, and guide us as friends along the spiritual path. It is for this reason that they are ultimate objects of refuge.

When contemplating our motivation for taking refuge, we must make sure that it is based on pure renunciation. It is only by practicing and maintaining pure moral conduct that we can stop the increase of defilements; this, therefore, is the foundation of Dharma practice. We must renounce all rebirth in samsara, not just rebirth in lower realms. All sensual happiness is a cause for suffering; any close friendship or attraction is really of the nature of suffering. We must investigate and apply the right antidote to cut this merciless cycling in samsara. Once pure renunciation is attained, we can gain meditative equipoise through the practice of concentration. Using this meditative equipoise, we can directly see the nontrue existence of self and all phenomena, and thereby gain liberation. Refuge and renunciation are the ground for this achievement. Without them it cannot be attained.

Just as correct motivation is crucial to the success of any practice, pure dedication is indispensable also. Chöd is the same as any other practice in this regard. We should know the reasons for this through *lamrim*[47] teachings, whether we are of the Gelug tradition or not. Developing pure motivation and correctly dedicating practice for the sake of the enlightenment of all sentient beings accumulates the merit to attain spontaneous, actual bodhichitta.

It is especially important in Chöd practice to maintain motivation with pure renunciation, pure bodhichitta, and the selfless generation of wisdom realizing emptiness. Giving our bodies to the spirits is the fundamental perfection practice of generosity upon which all other perfections are based. Offering our bodies transformed into nectar to the visualized and invoked field of merit gathers the two accumulations of merit and wisdom. Bodhichitta motivation gathers the accumulation of merit for attaining rupakaya, the form bodies, of Buddha. Realizing that giver, given, and recipient are all empty of inherent existence gathers the accumulation of transcendental wisdom for attaining dharmakaya, the truth body of Buddha.

If we train in *lamrim*, it is not necessary to meditate upon correct motivation extensively every time we engage in the practice of Chöd, because we can generate pure motivation by recollecting those teachings. It is particularly helpful to regard all appearances as dreams. We would never be attached to our dreams, so why be attached to appearances? If we are not mindful of the dreamlike nature of existence, and if we do not remember death, our actions become negative karma. Attachment to our bodies and our lives, our relatives and friends, entails that our actions of body, speech, and mind are negative. The antidote to this is to remember always the nearness of death and the dreamlike nature of this transitory life. Remembering "dream and death" morning, noon, and night is the expeditious way to maintain pure motivation for Chöd practice. With these two recollections, we should seek to liberate all beings and take them to enlightenment wherever we go. It is important to have compassionate awareness at all times, and to sustain great faith and confidence in our guru and dharma friends. In general, we should learn from all beings we meet, regarding them as manifestations of the guru's wisdom, but in particular we should look for, and learn from, the good qualities of our friends in Dharma.

The basis for the practice of Chöd thus refers to the motivation of the practitioner. Without motivation of pure renunciation of samsaric existence and pure bodhichitta, the practice of Chöd will not be pure, and may even be harmful.

ADVICE ON PRACTICE

If we are intending to practice Chöd outdoors, there are certain preliminary practices to be done relating to the site. In Tibet, some practitioners traveled to a hundred different springs to do this practice, but this requires a special empowerment called *Seven Days in Fearsome Sites*.[48] After receiving this, the disciple would leave for traveling Chöd retreat carrying all that was required, including a tent and a drum. The practitioner would spend one night at each site before moving to the next, in this way completing a hundred sites.[49]

When going to a fearsome place, or going on the "hundred springs retreat,"[50] there may occur various violent or seductive appearances caused by spirits. In order to remove these obstacles, we should apply proper motivation and any of the "four ways of walking": (1) "walking like a brave tiger," (2) "walking like Vajrayogini's heel steps," (3) "walking like a coiling black snake," and (4) "walking like the sky-goers' dance." These "walkings" are metaphors for four different attitudes, and one should bear one of these attitudes while going to the springs. For "walking like a brave tiger" and "walking like the sky-goers' dance," generate yourself as Heruka Chakrasamvara and hold divine pride of being the deity. For "walking like Vajrayogini's heel steps" and "walking like a coiling black snake," one generates as Vajrayogini, holding her divine pride.

When you arrive at the place, it is advisable to perform the "three overwhelmings"[51] to prevent deceitful appearances caused by mundane spirits and ghosts. First, right after arriving at the place and before doing anything, sit down and meditate on emptiness for a while. After that, set up your tent and, if there is water nearby, drink a few mouthfuls. If there is a tree nearby, gently pull its branches a few times. Finally, look for a small stone on some flat ground, and put it beneath your meditation cushion. Do not dig the soil or pollute it or any water nearby. Again, meditate briefly on emptiness of inherent existence of self and all phenomena as deeply as possible. After arising from emptiness meditation, open your eyes and look carefully with wide-opened eyes up into the sky, into the space around you, and down at the ground as you recite PHAT a few times. When you engage in the practice, try to sit in the seven-point posture of Buddha Vairochana.

Then visualize that your body has transformed into the shape of a stupa, huge and vast as Mount Meru. You should regard your stupa-shaped body as the synthesis of all gurus, yidams, buddhas, and dharma protectors. Visualize that the entire ground has been pressed down and is covered under the stupa of your body. Think that there is no longer any ordinary earth or stone remaining, but that the entire area is pervaded by your stupa-body. [52]

With firm determination, meditate on bodhichitta, reflecting that you have come to this place to dedicate your body to all sentient beings. Remember that all the spirits have been our kind mothers in previous lifetimes, whatever their appearances and actions now.

It is at this point that we meditate upon the three principal paths prior to the actual session of Chöd practice. From beginingless time up to the present, sentient beings have been controlled by their self-grasping attitude, due to which they are born in samsara, against their will, over and over again. Real sensitivity and empathy are indispensable to generating pure compassion unable to bear the desperate condition of beings caught in samasara. Hold the strong aspiration, "I shall not move from this spot until I liberate sentient beings onto the path of buddhahood!" Sacrifice your body to the spirits for their temporary benefit, with the pure motivation to lead them from suffering to enlightenment. The practice of Chöd repays the infinite kindness of all mother sentient beings. The foregoing instructions are to be implemented by practitioners going out to fearsome places to practice Chöd. Nevertheless, generating proper motivation before the actual body of the sadhana is necessary whether you are practicing indoors or out. If you go to a cemetery or frightening place, go by means of the four modes with the proper motivation. Do not think, "Soon I will be frightened or be eaten by spirits!" because you should *already* see your body as a corpse, and your mind as the corpse-bearer. When the body is thus taken by the mind to a frightful place, you should regard the place as a cemetery, a charnel ground of frightening appearance. You should think that your body is being taken to be eaten by spirits, just as jackals devour a carcass. Thus, going by means of the four modes means: (1) regarding the body as a corpse; (2) regarding the mind as the corpse-bearer; (3) regarding the fearsome place as a charnel ground; and (4) regarding the ghosts and spirits as jackals. Nyamay Gyalthangpa, a great Chöd master who composed a Chöd text, taught this "going by means of the four modes." All of these methods help to eliminate possible interferences.

When you begin your Chöd practice, set your mind in detachment from this life. Do not, for instance, expect that by practicing Chöd you'll gain fame and prosperity. Neither harbor attachment to the samsaric world nor seek good rebirths through your Chöd practice. In addition, Chöd practitioners must maintain unshakable faith in their gurus and dharma friends. The relationship between dharma friends is established when they receive teachings from a guru together. Practitioners receive the teachings after listening to them and receiving commitments to observe. No dharma student is completely lacking in good qualities, nor lacks a single virtuous quality at the level of his or her particular mental capacity. We need to acknowledge their qualities, respecting and rejoicing in them, thinking that it is really wonderful that they have such commitments and qualities. When we examine ourselves we find that it is difficult to observe commitments. The same is true for our dharma friends, but don't get discouraged; we are all striving in the same path. Therefore, we must remain faithful to our dharma friends. When we recite the verses of request, such as in the Chöd Ganachakra Sadhana, they include seeking blessings from our dharma friends.

While preparing motivation, remember that all phenomena are merely imputed by name and label, and so lack inherent existence. We must discover the inter-relationship between emptiness of inherent existence and dependent arising, and view all things and events as being like dreams, because they do not exist in the manner in which they appear to our minds. Remember the truth of the law of karma, and cultivate love and compassion for the ghosts and spirits. Hold a very strong determination to liberate the ghosts and spirits of that place during that very session upon the cushion. With such a motivation we should go to frightful places.

✒ Preliminary Practices of Chöd

THE SESSION begins with four preliminary practices. These are:

1. Going for refuge and generating bodhichitta
2. Guru Yoga, gateway to empowering blessings
3. Accumulating merit through the seven-limb prayer and offering of mandala
4. Purification of obscurations and unwholesome actions through the descent of nectar from AH

GOING FOR REFUGE AND GENERATING BODHICHITTA

When visualizing the objects of refuge, we should do so in accordance with the *Guru Puja* field for the accumulation of merit. This visualized field of merit is good for all practices. We should try to use this whenever we can, so that we can memorize its clear appearance. Depending on what practice we are doing, however, we need to change the aspect of the central object of refuge. In *Guru Puja* it is Je Tsongkhapa. In Chöd practice, it is Machig Labdrön and the four dakinis,[53] omitting the wish-fulfilling tree and the ocean of milk. In general, we should study teachings on *Guru Puja* most carefully. It is our most blessed guru yoga, and the most extensive.

In order to practice Chöd, we must receive the empowerment and oral transmission. The authentic blessings of the practice arise from this authorization, and are deepened by the correct chanting and playing of the Chöd damaru. Studying these skills of chanting and playing, training in them, and finally using them, is very beneficial and effective. We should learn the correct visualizations, authentic chant melodies and style of damaru playing from the start.

Visualize the objects of refuge carefully and mindfully. In the space before you is a glorious high spacious throne raised by eight snow lions. Upon this throne is a thousand-petal multicolored lotus (or you can visualize a four-petal lotus). In the middle of the lotus, visualize a moon disc upon which Machig Labdrön stands. She is white, in dancing posture, adorned with white silk. She holds a damaru of red wood and a bell of white silver. The deity should always be regarded as embodying your guru. Without this constant recollection, there will be no success in your practice.

Above the head of Machig Labdrön is Buddha Vajradhara, and at her heart is the wisdom being, Great Mother Prajnaparamita. The Great Mother is yellow with four arms[54] and has a blue HUM at her heart, the concentration being, symbolizing dharmakaya. From the HUM emanate many-colored wisdom lights.

On the petals of the lotus around Machig Labdrön, you can visualize Guhyasamaja on the right, Yamantaka on the left, Chakrasamvara behind, and Hevajra in front.[55] Surrounding the lotus in eleven tiers are the root and lineage gurus, the deities of Tantra, the buddhas, bodhisattvas, and so forth. In front of each one you should visualize a Prajnaparamita Sutra, signifying complete understanding of dharma. These texts should be regarded as wisdom speech and the dharma refuge. Finally, there are the dharma protectors.

All of the visualized field of merit should be perceived as smiling at you and granting you their blessings due to your taking refuge in them, and your generation of pure bodhichitta.

Around and in front of you, visualize other beings taking refuge and generating bodhichitta. In front of you are the local spirits, spirits who cause you harm, and enemies. On your right is your father; on your left is your mother. Your family and friends surround you. Extending into the directions around and behind you are all sentient beings, in human form. You should think that they can all speak and understand Dharma, and that they have all generated pure motivation.

With stable visualization of the field of merit, we must meditate to collect the causes of fearlessness: faith and love. By contemplating how all
sentient beings are trapped in samsara, we generate pure renunciation on
their behalf. Fearlessness comes from this renunciation of samsara. Perceiving the objects of refuge, we recognize that they are valid objects of
faith because of their power to overcome samsara. If we have correct faith,
there is no way we cannot achieve our aims. Correct faith leads to the
confidence to overcome all obstacles. Finally, by recalling how all sentient
beings are suffering in the prison of samsara, we cultivate loving-kindness
and compassion, wishing to save them from continuous suffering.

While engaged in Chöd practice, we will not have a lot of time to visualize everything precisely, so we should familiarize ourselves with the visualizations and, at that time, briefly recall them as best we can. What is
important, however, is to recognize definitely the Buddha Jewel, the
Dharma Jewel, and the Sangha Jewel, and to take refuge in them on behalf
of all suffering sentient beings. In particular, we are taking unshakable
refuge in Machig Labdrön.

After taking refuge and generating the aspiring and engaging forms of
bodhichitta,[56] we should visualize tubes of light radiating from the objects
of refuge to our hearts, and to the hearts of all beings visualized around
and in front of us. Through these light tubes, nectar flows down from
the objects of refuge, purifying all negativities, especially negativities
against the refuge vows. As the lights and nectars again descend to us and
all beings, we should think that all of our good qualities are increased,
and that we are empowered by the blessings of the objects of refuge. As
the light and nectar descend a third time, think very strongly that we and
all sentient beings have come forever under the protection of the Three
Jewels.

The field of merit then dissolves into light and is absorbed into Machig
Labdrön, who is regarded as the embodiment of all objects of refuge. She
comes to the crown of the head and descends to the heart, where she dissolves in bliss. Then visualize all appearances dissolving into light and
absorbing into your body. Your body then dissolves into light and disappears into emptiness. Meditate upon this emptiness as ultimate refuge.

GURU YOGA, GATEWAY TO EMPOWERING BLESSINGS

If we wish, we can visualize the previous field of merit for the guru yoga, also. The principal figure in the visualization can be Je Tsongkhapa, Machig Labdrön, or Vajrayogini.[57] Whichever we choose, the deity must be regarded as inseparable from the guru.

The field of merit is visualized as before, but with the addition that each guru, yidam, buddha, and so forth has the five syllables[58] marking their bodies and the Prajnaparamita volume in front of them. We then invoke the actual wisdom beings by visualizing light emanating from the HUM at their hearts. The wisdom beings merge with the visualized field, and we hold the clear awareness that they are all of the same essence, that of the Guru Buddha.

Visualize yourself as a huge, smooth-skinned being with a lotus and sun disc a few inches above the crown of your head. On the sun disc, Machig Labdrön dances in the aspect of Vajravarahi. She should be regarded as of a nature inseparable from your root guru. There are many different aspects of Vajravarahi, some with two faces.[59] Here, visualize Vajravarahi in her usual aspect as the red dancing dakini holding curved knife and skull-cup. A khatvanga rests against her left shoulder. She has loose hair, and peace radiates from the pores of her body. She has a somewhat wrathful expression, her forehead is wrinkled, but she is smiling. She is adorned with the bone ornaments, a crown of skulls, necklaces, bracelets, anklets, and an apron of bone.

Generally speaking, there are six bone ornaments, cemetery ashes being the sixth, but the female wisdom aspect does not have more than five. For example, Yamantaka has an extremely wrathful form, and has blue ashes from the charnel grounds abundantly scattered on his body, whereas Heruka, who is wrathful with great desire, has such ashes, but only in small patches. Related to this point, Yamantaka also has white ash dots to increase the white elements in the body, thereby increasing great bliss. Both of these male deities have melted fat applied to their bodies. Female deities do not usually have ashes or melted fat on their bodies.

In general, wrathful deities should be visualized completely enveloped in transcendental wisdom fire. This is done in order to increase bliss within us, and to burn away all obstacles and obscurations to accomplishing the deity.

After visualizing Vajravarahi clearly, visualize also the three syllables at her three places. From the HUM at her heart, light radiates and invites all peaceful and wrathful Vajrayoginis from their natural abode in dharmakaya. As dharmakaya is omnipresent, whenever someone generates a pure intention to invoke the deity from dharmakaya, the deity will always come there in a physical form.

At this point we should contemplate the correct meaning of "guru yoga." Our guru is the only source of Buddha's blessings, and, therefore, of enlightenment. There are Buddhas present before all sentient beings, but, due to their karmic obscurations, beings cannot see them. Because of this, the Buddhas manifest as gurus. If we rely upon the guru with this proper understanding, wherever we go or whatever we do, we will be successful.

When beings become enlightened, their mental continuums become the same. Only when beings are not enlightened can their mental continuums be described as different. Put another way, in the Vajrayana it states that if we attain one yidam deity, we attain all of them. The same is said in the Paramitayana. To realize one high deity is to realize all high deities. The following analogy may prove useful. The waters from different rivers have similar fish in them. When these rivers flow into the ocean, no one can tell which river each fish came from. And, just as the vast ocean can support large numbers of beings, similarly, when we become enlightened, we can benefit all beings. The guru represents this tremendous achievement.

Even though the sun's rays are bright, they can only ignite fire when a magnifying glass is present. The guru is like a magnifying glass for the blessings of Buddha. Visualizing the guru in the form of a deity makes the blessings more powerful. We should not visualize the guru in ordinary aspect, or as a statue, but as a real, living deity with all the qualities of Buddha's body, speech and mind.

It is very beneficial to know all the different qualities of Buddha. If we do, our life spans will be prolonged. We should therefore come to know all of the major and minor signs of a Buddha's body. Buddha's speech is very melodious and is able to liberate all beings instantaneously. It is not like ordinary speech, but is like the different deities of the Sanskrit alphabet—A, AA, I, II, and so on. Buddha's mind knows all phenomena completely and has limitless love for all beings. The power of Buddha's mind is incomparable. Whatever beings think or do is known by Buddha's mind. The many qualities of Buddha's divine activities can only be comprehended gradually, just as a pot cannot hold all rainfall at once. In order to gain this understanding and actualize such qualities, we must complete the accumulations of merit and wisdom.

While viewing the guru as Buddha, meditate on Buddha's qualities very carefully. A dream body is not a physical body. In the same way, the guru's body is not tangible or solid in any way; it is like a reflection in a mirror. Those who saw the body of Shakyamuni Buddha said that it was like candlelight that one could see but not touch. In this way we should visualize the guru as the deity, the embodiment of all buddhas and bodhisattvas. In a similar way, the guru's speech gives continual teachings although we may not be able to hear it at present. The guru's mind and the Buddha's mind are the same—omniscient and totally compassionate.

The major contemplation of Guru Yoga, therefore, is to see the visualized deity as the guru unshakably seated in dharmakaya, while simultaneously benefiting all sentient beings. Visualize Guru Vajravarahi emanating blissful light that brings all beings to enlightenment. In addition, we can invoke all the divine beings, the "wisdom beings," and absorb them into our guru. If we have total faith that the guru deity possesses all qualities, it is unnecessary to invoke the wisdom beings. If we do not have this faith, however, invocation is necessary. For most people, fewer than a thousand invocations will not bring successful results. Those with more merit can visualize the entire universe as part of the divine body of the guru. It is therefore very important to understand clearly how to invoke the deity. When we make the invocation, all the wisdom beings merge with the deity, from the top, like rain, from the sides, like clouds, and, from the bottom, like vapor. After we have done this we visualize clearly and powerfully that Vajravarahi is the synthesis of all buddhas and bodhisattvas.

From the HUM at Vajravarahi's heart, light radiates to the ten directions once more. This light eliminates all harm, spirit possession, and personal obstacles. Simultaneously, this light invites all sentient beings, including evildoers and spirits. They come and surround us like swans coming to a lake. These beings all look at each other very happily. There is no need for binding mantras like DZA HUM BAM HO. All these beings pay great homage to Vajravarahi. They fold their hands at their hearts, perform the seven-limb prayer, and make mandala offerings along with us. This completes the guru yoga practice.

ACCUMULATING MERIT THROUGH SEVEN-LIMB PRAYER AND MANDALA OFFERING

Seven-limb prayer consists of the following:

(1) homage
(2) offerings
(3) confession
(4) rejoicing
(5) requesting teachings
(6) requesting not passing into nirvana
(7) dedication

First, we pay homage by way of expressing the good qualities of Guru Vajravarahi. We should think that all the beings surrounding us recite the homage and the following prayers along with us. We can also recite the eight-line praise of Vajravarahi here.

Offerings are next. These are of four types: outer, inner, secret and suchness. Outer offerings are of waters, flowers and so forth. These have no consciousness and are therefore termed "outer," or "external."

Inner offerings are offerings of the sense consciousnesses, visualized as offering goddesses each holding symbols of their particular sense offerings. These goddesses are of form (white), of sound (blue), of smell (yellow), of taste (red), and of touch (green). It is very important to visualize as imaginatively as possible; for example, the form goddesses hold up mirrors in which the whole universe is reflected, the sound goddesses make beautiful music, the goddesses of fragrance make the scent of perfume pervasive and so on. All offerings should be regarded as perfect, with many goddesses pervading all of space. This is very effective for accumulating merit. If we do this correctly, we will feel as if there is no room to make any other offerings! Visualize the offerings as Dharma arising in form and then returning to dharmakaya. It is by making offerings of form, for example, that the eyes are pleased. Therefore an inner offering to the eye is made. The deity has no need of it, but visualizing it is beneficial to *us*.

The secret offering is offering of consort to the deity and thereby offering the four joys so that bliss may be developed. The offering of suchness follows. We recall that the nature of those previous offerings' three spheres—the giver, the given, and the receiver—are empty of true existence. By meditating on this emptiness with a mind of bliss, we make the offering of suchness to Vajravarahi. This helps us to realize the union of bliss and emptiness.

Next of the seven limbs is confession. We must confess all of our negative actions of body, speech and mind to Guru Vajravarahi. Each of the ten nonvirtuous actions must be confessed because we have committed all of them over the course of our countless lifetimes. We must admit everything with honesty to Vajravarahi, applying the four opponent powers. Visualizing Vajravarahi is *reliance*. We then develop *regret* for the nonvirtuous actions we have done, followed by the *vow* not to repeat such actions in the future. Finally, *remedial action,* here, is the confession you are making. It is important to understand what is actually being confessed at this time. Ultimately, negative actions do not exist. They do exist conventionally, in the manner of a dream. It is these conventionally existent negative actions that are confessed to Vajravarahi. "Dream" does not mean "totally false" in this context. Dreams can produce happiness or suffering for us in the waking state. This means that the dream truly occurred; it had an effect. "Conventional" negative actions are "true" in this sense.

After confession comes *rejoicing.* This means rejoicing in the wholesome actions of ourselves and of others. Ultimately, they do not exist, but conventionally, they do exist. In general we should admire the virtuous actions of past, present, and future Buddhas, all sentient beings and ourselves. Rejoice especially in the actions of holy, realized beings. As all actions are like a dream, it is easy to rejoice in them. Despite their dreamlike nature, actions are still subject to the infallible law of cause and effect. Ultimately, all phenomena are nontruly existent, but, relatively speaking, the law of karma is inevitable. In this way we should think that all actions are like dreams.

Rejoicing in the actions of others is the major antidote to jealousy. When we admire the virtuous deeds of ourselves and of others, a great increase of merit is created. Jealousy is very harmful, and must be destroyed by rejoicing. If we rejoice in the virtue of someone whose understanding is less than our own, we gain greater merit than that person. If we rejoice in the merit of someone with understanding equal to ours, we gain equal merit. If we rejoice in the realization or virtue of someone more highly realized than we are, we accumulate some fraction of the merit that they do. We must rejoice in virtue because we have taken bodhisattva vows. If other beings practice well it helps us; therefore we should rejoice in their positive actions. This is the easiest way to accumulate merit with little hardship. With consistent effort the practice of rejoicing becomes very powerful and is greatly praised by many masters.

The request for teachings is made by requesting Guru Vajravarahi to turn the wheel of all three vehicles. Three interpretations of the three vehicles can be presented. The three vehicles are the outer, inner, and secret. These could be regarded as the Hinayana, Bodhisattvayana, and Tantrayana. Another interpretation could be Paramitayana, the lower Tantras, and the higher Tantras. According to Tantra, the three vehicles are Kriya and Charya Tantras, the Yoga Tantras, and the Maha-anuttarayoga Tantras. Whatever the vehicle, it should be remembered that realizing "non-inherent existence" is the main path reaching enlightenment. The request for teachings is made on behalf of all sentient beings bound in samsara.

The request not to pass into nirvana is made to Guru Vajravarahi as the essence of all buddhas and bodhisattvas, imploring all the holy beings not to pass into nirvana until all sentient beings have realized buddhahood.

Having accumulated merit, we must dedicate properly. Any virtuous action requires correct dedication. Dedication is the vehicle that takes us to enlightenment. We should dedicate all our virtuous actions to the attainment of buddhahood for the sake of all sentient beings.

The seven-limb prayer section begins with PHAT. This sacred word helps to remind us of the nontrue existence of all phenomena. It is for this reason that it appears at the beginning of the prayer section and else-where in the text of the sadhana. Because every phenomenon is empty, it is easy to understand how all phenomena are dependent arisings. If a person were truly existent from his or her own side, it would be impossible to become free of samsara; practicing Dharma would be meaningless. In the same way, if nirvana were truly existent from its own side, it would not be possible to attain it or to gather the causes for its attainment.

When we have completed the dedication, we should visualize being purified by Guru Vajravarahi. From the heart of Guru Vajravarahi above us, lights and nectars descend into our bodies, purifying all negativities and filling us with joy. Our bodies become totally pure and clear as glass. The lights and nectars radiating from Guru Vajravarahi also purify all sentient beings around us in the same way.

Following the purification meditation, offer the inner mandala to the deity. Begin by saying PHAT, remembering that all phenomena are non-inherently existent. Visualize your body as vast, white, fat and oily. Within this body, visualize the central channel extending from the navel to the crown of the head. It is very straight, white outside and red inside. The lower tip extends four finger-widths below the navel. There is no need to visualize the navel chakra for this meditation.

At the navel is the mind in the form of a reddish-white drop, sparkling and lightweight, about to ascend the central channel. The mind-drop wishes to melt into the heart of Guru Vajravarahi above the crown of the head. Do not think that your mind is in your head looking down on this. Be convinced that your mind is within the mind-drop, looking upwards, and yearning to unite with Mother Vajravarahi.

Recite PHAT five times in order to unite with Mother Vajravarahi. With each recitation the mind-drop ascends first to the heart, then to the throat, then to the crown of the head. With the fourth PHAT, the mind-drop ascends into the heart of Guru Vajravarahi, and, with the final PHAT, our former bodies fall to the ground. The body should be viewed as very exten-sive, vast as Mount Meru. Realize that with all previous bodies in count-less rebirths, you have accomplished nothing meaningful, but that now you have this wonderful opportunity to extract a meaningful essence from your now discarded base of a body.

Then, from the blissful heart of Guru Vajravarahi, our minds emanate as a green action dakini holding a curved knife. We should visualize this very strongly while uttering PHAT once more. The dakini lands near the corpse, and, with the curved knife, splits the body from the crown to the navel, shouting PHAT as she does so. The dismemberment of the body proceeds at each stage accompanied by the utterance of PHAT. The right arm is severed, then the left arm. The right leg is severed, then the left. The skin is peeled back, bleeding, onto the ground. Our minds as action dakinis are very pleased at these opportunities to make inner offerings.

With the intention to make this bodily basis a meaningful offering, we should say PHAT once more, and visualize the skin transforming into a golden ground as vast as the universe. At this point we offer the mandala chanting slowly and melodiously. By chanting slowly, we can visualize precisely, and remember the meaning clearly. We should also hold the Chöd damaru in front of us with both hands, and upon it visualize the inner mandala offering as vast as the universe. There must be no sense of the skin being anywhere else than upon the damaru, which is now acting as the inner mandala base; yet the damaru is now perceived as tremendous in extent. A hundred thousand universes could fit upon it.

Chanting slowly and precisely, the inner mandala offering is made by transforming the bodily basis into a pure offering to the field of merit. Our blood is sprinkled onto the ground by the action dakini, and immediately transforms into nectar. The dakini then takes all the internal organs and so on, beginning with the intestines, which she arranges and transforms into the ring of mountains at the circumference of the mandala. The four limbs become the four continents, the spine becomes Mount Meru, and the head becomes the mansion of Indra on its summit. The two eyes become the sun and moon, the two ears become parasol and victory banner. The remainder becomes the inexhaustible wealth of humans and devas.

Saying PHAT once more, we view this magnificent inner mandala offering as non-inherently existent, and cut all attachment to its appearance. This effects a cutting of attachment to possessions and severance of self-grasping. With a pure motivation of nonattachment, we then offer the mandala to the gurus, yidams, buddhas, bodhisattvas and protectors, requesting their blessings. It is termed an inner mandala because the basis of this mandala was previously held in the continuum of a human being.

The purpose of meditation on Chöd is to perfect the realizations of conventional and ultimate bodhichitta. Chöd practice itself can be regarded as a continual purification practice that brings these two realizations. Yet in order to practice Chöd, we must gain realization of the three principal paths: renunciation, bodhichitta, and the correct view of emptiness, as explained by Je Tsongkhapa. Chöd practice is like an ornament to the three principal paths. Je Rinpoche said that the three principal paths are the roots. Without them we cannot sustain the branches of tantric practice that deal with the channels, winds, and drops of the completion stage. With firm roots, such advanced practices will be fruitful.

Whenever we practice Chöd, we need bodhichitta motivation at the very least. We must contemplate very carefully why we are practicing Chöd before we start to engage in the practice. Following that contemplation, we engage in "internal Chöd," or "internal cutting." This is another name for generating bodhichitta in the Chöd system. In general, it should be done before beginning the sadhana itself and should be recollected during the inner mandala offering and during the requests to the gurus for blessings.

There are two ways of generating bodhichitta in the "internal Chöd" practice: in accordance with *lamrim* meditations, and in accordance with a special Chöd meditation on bodhichitta.

Without *lamrim* practice, Dharma practitioners can do nothing. It is so important. At present we are as if blind—we do not know what to practice and what to abandon. Our lives are full of anger and aggressive reactions. Anger is extremely dangerous. It destroys wholesome goals of practice and previously accumulated merit. Not knowing what is to be abandoned, we are tied to samsara by desirous attachment to objects of the five senses—forms, sounds, smells, tastes, and tactile sensations. All mother beings[60] are equal in that all are bound in samsara by attachment's chains and are carried helplessly away by the four great rivers of birth, aging, sickness, and death. Not knowing what is to be practiced, we cannot escape from this terror.

In order to generate bodhichitta according to *lamrim,* we must confront this situation clearly, and, using our powers of reason, come to definite decisions. First, we must see that our negative actions arise due to prejudice and erroneous judgments. The discrimination that labels some as "friends" and others as "enemies" must be perceived as at the root of our problems. We need to see that we label people and things in terms of our own desires, our own wishes. These wishes are transitory. The labeled objects are, themselves, impermanent. Such labeling is therefore very confused and false, yet it persists, and we continue to create suffering for ourselves. To avoid this, we need to develop equanimity for all beings suffering in samsara, tossed to and fro by their fleeting delusions, just like ourselves.

Secondly, we meditate on all beings as having been our mothers in previous lifetimes. We cannot point to any beginning of our lifetimes in the various types of births—miracle, heat and moisture, egg, or womb. Neither can we point to any being that has not been our mother countless times.

We follow this meditation by considering the kindness of mothers. To do this, we meditate on our present mother's kindness to us and extend the feeling of gratitude that arises towards all beings we meet. Returning the kindness shown us by our mothers accumulates vast merit. In any situation that may present itself, we should determine to repay the kindness of all sentient beings. Whatever their appearance or actions, they have all been our kind mothers in previous lifetimes. Due to his having abused his mother in a previous lifetime, Buddha's disciple Maudgalyayana experienced a painful ripening of his karma. He was renowned for his attainment of siddhis and as a teacher, but once, with other disciples of Buddha, he was insulted and attacked by a group of non-Buddhists. The other Buddhists escaped, but Maudgalyayana could not do so. Even his ability to fly deserted him, and he received a severe beating. Later, when questioned about this occurrence, he replied that the beating and temporary loss of his siddhis had been due to his having abused his mother in a previous life. This was the ripened effect of that grievous action. In general, there are many harmful karmic effects associated with abuse, neglect, or any negative action towards our parents. This is because our parents have been so kind to us in the past.

We continue this *lamrim* meditation for developing bodhichitta by meditating on loving-kindness that dearly cherishes others, holding the determination to selflessly bring happiness to others. We next shift to great compassion meditation. This is the wish to free all mother sentient beings from their miseries by taking on their sufferings. Recognition of our responsibility to free all sentient beings from samsaric suffering is the next meditation, called "superior intention." Considering our superior intentions and the ability to fulfill them, we realize that only the attainment of buddhahood can bring the ability to free all sentient beings from samsara. Buddhahood is seen as the fulfillment of both one's own and others' purposes. It enables us to completely repay the kindness that all mother sentient beings have shown us. The strong wish to attain buddhahood as quickly as possible in order to help all mother sentient beings escape from samsaric misery is conventional bodhichitta, the altruistic aspiration for enlightenment.

This *lamrim* bodhichitta meditation is usually called the "sevenfold cause-and-effect instruction," not including equanimity as the first meditation. It is sometimes held that this is because bodhichitta is the "effect" of the previous six "causal" meditations, while another interpretation is that each meditation in the sequence is an "effect" of the preceding meditation. Whichever interpretation is accepted, it is important that generation of equanimity for all—friend, foe, and stranger—remains as the foundation.

The second way of generating bodhichitta in the "internal Chöd" practice is to focus one's attention on this present rebirth as a human being, and contemplate that none of our countless previous bodies generated any ultimate fruit, any meaningful realization. Realizing this, determine to make the most of this human rebirth right now, from this very moment. Strongly desire to "extract the essence" from this life, thinking, "this is my only opportunity to benefit mother sentient beings, because there is no certainty that I'll again find a fully endowed human rebirth." For these reasons we decide, without hope or fear, to give our bodies to satisfy all beings materially, and to give holy Dharma to satisfy all beings spiritually. This is the special Chöd meditation on bodhichitta, based on contemplation of the precious human rebirth.

Unless we meditate on bodhichitta, the door to Mahayana practice, we will remain "ordinary" until our "ordinary" deaths. To develop bodhichitta requires effort and blessings. We request the lineage gurus of Chöd for blessings. In order to make the correct effort, however, we must diligently practice *lamrim* meditation and the precious *lojong,* or mind training instructions. From the very beginning of practice, we must persevere in generating a mind controlled with correct motivation. To control the mind requires an effort that is sustained and properly directed. The proper direction is bodhichitta motivation.

PURIFYING OBSTRUCTIONS AND NONVIRTUE THROUGH THE DESCENT OF NECTAR FROM AH

Purification practice in this Chöd system has two parts: the request to the lineage gurus, and the actual descent of nectar from the syllable AH.

Following the text of the sadhana, the first three stanzas of request are to the gurus of the distant lineage. The distant lineage has two aspects: that of profound view, and that of vastness. The first two stanzas are to the gurus of profound view, the "father" and "mother" Chöd lineages, respectively. The third stanza is to the gurus of the lineage of method or vastness. The requests to the lineage gurus, from the fourth stanza onwards, are to the lineage gurus of the close lineage, beginning with Buddha Vajradhara.

There are different systems of requesting blessings. If we do it elaborately, after each guru's name we can recite the prayer to the Mahamudra lineage gurus:[61]

> Please bless me to sever self-grasping's bondage,
> To train in love, compassion and bodhichitta,
> And, through the Mahamudra path of union,
> Quickly attain supreme enlightenment!

It is very beneficial to do this even though it takes time. Another way is to make requests to each guru residing in his or her own abode, and then add the above Mahamudra prayer only once at the very end. For example, we recite:

In Akanishta Dharma Palace,
All pervasive Vajradhara, I beseech!
In mansion of great bliss Dharmakaya,
Bhagavati Vajravarahi, I beseech!
At the Five-peaked Mountain of China,
Manjushri, Treasure of Wisdom, I beseech!
In Manjushri's practice mandala,
Revered Pawo Dorje, I beseech!
At peerless glorious Ganden Mountain
Conqueror Losang Dragpa, I beseech![62]

It is helpful to tame the mind if we recite in this way for all the lineage gurus.

The short way of requesting is in accordance with the text of the sadhana. From the fourth stanza of the lineage prayer onwards, gurus of the "blessed close lineage" are mentioned. The fifth stanza includes reference to the "vajra brothers" who held the lineage of the empowerment, commentary, and transmission of this Chöd system. After the first Panchen Lama and his close disciples come the lineage gurus of the empowerment and commentary. Trinle Chöpel was a great renunciant. Losang Namgyal was the writer of a widely used Chöd text, and the founder of Samdring Monastery in Kyirong. Yeshe Gyaltsen was tutor to the eighth Dalai Lama. Losang Chöjor was a blessed yogi. Yeshe Tenzin was also a lama of Samdring Monastery. Thubten Gyatso lived in a house in Lhasa called the Nyungne House. He held secret lineages. Yeshe Döndrub was a great geshe of Tharpa Chöling Monastery. Tenzin Khedrub was the author of this list of lineage gurus. Kelsang Khedrub was the next lineage guru. Jampel Lhundrub was the tutor of Dechen Nyingpo. Dechen Nyingpo was the actual name of Kyabje Phabongka.

Kyabje Phabongka had such vast qualities that it is difficult to comprehend them. Sincere and pure practitioners should consult the birth stories of this high lama. Je Phabongka was an emanation of Krishnapada. Krishnapada was a great mahasiddha, a scholar and realized being. Wherever he traveled he levitated, shaded by the canopy of a seven-tiered parasol and heralded by the sound of damarus.

With respect to the lineages of Heruka Chakrasamvara, there are three: of Krishnapada, Luipa, and Ghantapada. Of these three, the lineage of Krishnapada is most precious. He interpreted the hidden meanings of the Heruka Tantra like Vajradhara himself. It is very blessed to recite these sadhanas, yet nowadays people ignore them.

In his lifetime, Krishnapada did not manifest enlightenment. To the view of ordinary appearances, this was due to transgressing the words of Jalendhara, his guru. At one time, Krishnapada requested permission from Jalendhara to engage in the yogic conduct of an ascetic.[63] Krishnapada tried to demonstrate his attainment to his guru by causing fruit to fall from a tree by merely looking at it, but Jalendhara refused him permission, because he could not also return the fruit to the tree by just looking at it. A little later, Krishnapada again requested permission to engage in ascetic practice in order to perfect pure conduct. His guru told him to manifest as a tiger, go to a charnel ground, and swallow a corpse. Krishnapada achieved this but was unable to vomit up the corpse whole and restore it to life, so Jalendhara told him to do more meditation rather than pursue tantric conduct. Once more Krishnapada requested permission, and once more Jalendhara refused, but this time, Krishnapada went into solitary retreat in the forest without his guru's permission. Due to this transgression he did not attain enlightenment in his lifetime. He did not transgress as we do, but he transgressed enough not to show the manner of his attaining enlightenment in that lifetime.

Later in life, Krishnapada was in retreat in a cave, and was about to offer ganachakra outside his cave when a black man appeared and told him that *he* should preside over the offering ceremony. This man was actually Chakrasamvara, but Krishnapada did not recognize him and refused. Chakrasamvara then assumed his blue aspect, and flew away into the sky. Krishnapada was full of remorse and spontaneously composed a prayer to Chakrasamvara. This praise is often recited—at the end of the *Yoga of the Three Purifications*, for example—and is very blessed due to Krishnapada's vision.

On another occasion, Krishnapada and his disciples were traveling on the banks of the river Ganges. At a fording place they met a leprous woman whose hands were disfigured. She wished to cross the river and requested help. Krishnapada did not help her, but one of his disciples, the novice monk Kusali, felt great compassion for her and started to carry her across the river in his robe. In the middle of the river the leper woman transformed into Vajrayogini, and immediately transported the monk to the Pure Land of the Dakinis. Krishnapada was left on the bank of the river watching this.

When Krishnapada was passing away, he discovered that this had been due to the harm of a worldly dakini. Manifesting death, Krishnapada attained enlightenment in the bardo state. His closest disciple was Guhyapa, who is included in the Five-Deity Heruka lineage gurus. Guhyapa chased this dakini until he trapped her in a tree and "released" her.[64]

Je Phabongka was a reincarnation of the mahasiddha Krishnapada, but in another life he was a minister to a king named De-ngön-dawa. Sometimes stories of the lives of great masters do not contain explicit Dharma teachings, but they do reveal the workings of karma. An example of this is the text of the *Thirty-four Deeds* from the Jataka tales that is taught by the Ganden Tripas during the Great Prayer Festival.[65] Another such example is the story of Prince De-ngön-dawa.

Once there was a kingdom whose king, named King Kulenraja, was a manifestation of Avalokiteshvara, and whose queen, named Queen Matimaha, was an emanation of White Tara. The king's son was Prince De-ngön-dawa. The king also had four important religious ministers, and one main adviser named Tongpön Yamshe. Tongpön Yamshe wished his son, Laka Anna, to be friends with the prince. The king accepted this friendship, but the queen experienced several bad signs in her dreams and predicted that the sun would soon set. She said that the king's decision would be inauspicious. The king, however, replied that he could not change his decision. Approaching the king, the religious ministers also protested the close relationship between Laka Anna and the prince. Yet, when they saw Tongpön Yamshe seated beside the throne with a long sword at his side, they left without saying anything. Afraid of their opposition, Tongpön Yamshe persuaded the king that the religious ministers were plotting together, and the king had them arrested and imprisoned. The queen's protests at this saved them from execution for the time being.

The queen's father, King Losheka, who was an emanation of Vajrapani, told her that the people of the country were alarmed and infuriated by the condemnation of the religious ministers and by the actions of Tongpön Yamshe. The queen decided to send the ministers to the safety of her father's kingdom if she could arrange it. Worrying about her husband, her son, and the kingdom, she became very sick and passed away.King Kulen-raja was left distraught by his queen's death. In accordance with her wishes, he sent the ministers to King Losheka's kingdom. Rejecting them with anger, King Losheka predicted that only three of the four would be able to return home. Tongpön Yamshe then informed the king that his other queen had given gifts to the exiled ministers. On hearing this, the king became even angrier at what he saw as disloyalty and treachery, and violently attacked his other queen. Tongpön Yamshe was now in virtual control of the kingdom.

At this time Prince De-ngön-dawa was married to a devout princess named Sersangma, but remained a close friend of Laka Anna's. Together, De-ngön-dawa and Laka Anna received teachings on consciousness transference from a wandering yogi. Once they had become proficient in this practice, Laka Anna caught two birds and persuaded De-ngön-dawa to cross the river by using the transference practice. De-ngön-dawa agreed to this suggestion, and sent away their servants. Princess Sersangma was very alarmed, and Laka Anna threatened her and told her to remain quiet and return to the palace.

Using their transference practice, the two crossed the river as birds, but now Laka Anna's treachery became clear. He returned immediately and entered De-ngön-dawa's body, not his own. Then he destroyed his own former body and set off back to the palace. Everyone saw Prince De-ngön-dawa returning, not suspecting him to actually be Laka Anna. Princess Sersangma, however, felt strange in the presence of her husband. Her suspicions increased when "De-ngön-dawa" said that Laka Anna had drowned in the river. His father, Tongpön Yamshe, hearing this story, went mad with grief and threw himself from a high cliff.

De-ngön-dawa's actions began to make people suspicious of him. Princess Sersangma offered a text to him that her husband used to recite, but he was unable to read it. The princess left the palace soon afterwards in secret, and went to the mountains to meditate. She became a great practitioner, with many wild animals befriending her.

At this time, the king's other queen also left the palace in dismay. More and more suspicious, Laka Anna, in De-ngön-dawa's body, ordered all birds to be prevented from entering the palace and its grounds. As he was the prince, his orders were obeyed.

But what of the real prince? De-ngön-dawa, in the body of a bird, was confused by his friend's disappearance, and became afraid when he could not find any human bodies on the riverbank. That night he had to stay perched in a tree. During the night a voice came to him explaining what had happened. Knowing that he could not communicate as a bird, he waited many days until he could transfer his consciousness into the corpse of a cuckoo. One day he met a parrot who could speak both human and bird language. Together, they taught Dharma to other birds of the forest, the parrot acting as De-ngön-dawa's interpreter. In this way they helped many sentient beings.

In the same forest, Princess Sersangma was also teaching Dharma to the animals who befriended her. She wore leaves, and ate fruits and roots, practicing intensively. All the time she expected to see her husband as a bird or as a wild animal. This made her practice very powerful. Like her husband, she, too, helped many sentient beings.

Meanwhile, Laka Anna had gone mad with the fear of discovery and ordered the killing of all animals and birds in the forest so as to prevent the return of the real prince. The king was very alarmed at his son's behavior. Laka Anna had changed the shape of the palace and changed its color from white to black.

One day, Guru Vimalashri came into the forest and walked up to the cuckoo and parrot. Placing a spear in the ground, he caused the two birds to stay where they were. He recited PHAT, then some mantras, and PHAT again. He placed the spear on the parrot's head, and it immediately died. Looking up at the cuckoo-prince, who was very confused, he explained that he had just transferred the consciousness of Laka Anna to a pure land, and had then transferred the consciousness of the parrot to De-ngön-dawa's body back in the palace. He went on to say that the cuckoo-prince could best help others by remaining in that form and teaching Dharma in the forest. Everything happened just as Guru Vimalashri had said. The "new" De-ngön-dawa became king and looked after his subjects well. He invited the four religious ministers to return, but only three returned, one having died in the meantime. One of these returning ministers was a previous incarnation of Kyabje Phabongka.

There exists a biography of De-ngön-dawa that describes all these events in more detail.[66] De-ngön-dawa was a previous incarnation of Tapu Dorje Chang, and Princess Sersangma was a previous incarnation of the Tapu Dorje Chang's spiritual consort. When Tapu Dorje Chang was alive in Tibet, Laka Anna was also reborn in Tibet.

Kyabje Phabongka was also an emanation of Heruka Chakrasamvara, but degeneration of the times and jealousy of ordinary beings have made it difficult to become aware of his tremendous qualities. There are many biographies of Kyabje Phabongka that make his realized qualities very clear.

On one occasion he received teachings inside a stupa in which there was a statue. From that time on, the head of this statue became larger and larger from year to year. Every year a new hat had to be offered to it. I have seen this. Another time, when he was young, he received *lamrim* teachings from Dagpo Lama Jampel Lhundrub, and when the customary ritual for generation of bodhichitta was held at the end of the teachings, he actually generated bodhichitta. When this happened, Jampel Lhundrub ordered a throne to be set up for the young Phabongka. On hearing the Sevenfold Cause-and-Effect instructions for the first time, his mind was greatly moved, and he wept.

Kyabje Phabongka received teachings on secret mantra from Yab Rinpoche. At one time it was difficult to receive the Five-Deity Heruka and Body Mandala of Heruka in Tibet, but Kyabje Phabongka obtained and taught these practices.

Once, when returning to central Tibet, Kyabje Phabongka nearly died from eating poisonous food. He recovered, but his face was blackened for a time and scarred. These marks disappeared as soon as he reached his room at Ganden.

The thirteenth Dalai Lama requested Kyabje Phabongka to give the yearly *lamrim* teachings in 1923, instead of asking the Ganden throneholder, as was customary. Usually these teachings lasted seven days, but these lasted for eleven days. These were my first teachings from Kyabje Phabongka. Kyabje Trijang Dorje Chang was also present at these teachings.

When I was twelve [1916] I came from my home in Kham [eastern Tibet] to Ganden Monastery [central Tibet] to pursue training in the sutras and tantras, and there I met Kyabje Trijang Rinpoche for the first time. Kyabje Trijang Rinpoche was then sixteen. We became vajra brothers but I always remained his disciple. Our common tutor was my mother's uncle, Losang Tsultrim. When I praise the qualities of Kyabje Trijang Dorje Chang, it is out of faith, not attachment.

Once, returning from Chamdo, Kyabje Phabongka taught at a "dzong," a fortified monastery. A member of his audience had a vision of Kyabje Phabongka with four arms. On another occasion, teaching at Lhasa, thirty-two incarnate lamas attended his *lamrim* discourses. Tapu Dorje Chang traveled from Kham to Lhasa specifically to receive Dharma teachings from Kyabje Phabongka. Tapu Dorje Chang could hear statues of Avalokiteshvara and Tara speak, and saw visions of multi-armed yidams. Kyabje Phabongka was Tapu Dorje Chang's disciple also.

Once Kyabje Phabongka invoked the wisdom beings of Heruka's mandala to enter into a statue of Heruka Chakrasamvara. Heruka then offered nectar to Kyabje Phabongka, and prophesied that seven generations of his disciples would be protected by the body mandala of Heruka. Kyabje Trijang Dorje Chang is cared for by Heruka Chakrasamvara, as are his disciples.

Mochog Rinpoche was also a disciple of Dagpo Dorje Chang. In a previous life Mochog Rinpoche wrote *The Empowering Blessing of Speech,* and met Sharipa in India twice. In addition, he received the complete teachings on Mahakala from Rahula.

Kyabje Trijang Rinpoche and Kyabje Ling Rinpoche were tutors to His Holiness the Dalai Lama. They taught His Holiness everything from basic teachings to advanced levels. Kyabje Phabongka passed all of his lineages to Kyabje Trijang Dorje Chang. He often said this in discourses.

The purpose of this detailed exposition is to affirm the power of the lineage. If we lose faith in the lineage, we are lost. We should remember the biographies of past and present teachers.

We should never develop negative thoughts towards our root and lineage gurus. If we do not keep the commitments after having received teachings, this is a great downfall. After giving teachings, the guru should act in accordance with the capacities of disciples and their requests. If the disciples see the guru's actions as pure, this is proper practice. The guru should not act in contradictory ways.

After having made requests to the lineage gurus, we visualize light and nectar descending from them into ourselves, and into all the sentient beings around us. These lights and nectars purify all negativity, disease, and possession by spirits. The disease and negativity leaves our bodies in the form of black smoke. Possession by spirits leaves our bodies in the form of snakes, spiders, and insects. We should think strongly that empowering blessings have been granted by the objects of refuge for the realizations of the three principal paths. It is very important also to feel strongly that self-cherishing and self-grasping minds have been purified. As a result, our bodies are filled with blessings, our life spans are extended, and our understandings of both conventional and ultimate bodhichitta are increased.

The method for receiving purification and blessing is called "the descent of nectars from AH." At the heart of the main figure in the field of merit visualized before us is the wisdom being, Great Mother Prajnaparamita. At her heart is a moon disc and a yellow syllable AH. Reciting AH twenty-one times, light and nectar flows down from the AH and melts into our bodies and into the bodies of all sentient beings surrounding us. All obstacles and negativities are removed and purified. Blessings are received, and all beings attain the two bodhichittas. Playing the damaru, we recite AH twenty-one times, either seven AH's three times, or three AH's seven times,[67] ending with a single PHAT. It is important to do this slowly.

Kyabje Zong Rinpoche then took up his Chöd damaru and demonstrated the two ways in which the twenty-one AH's may be recited, accompanied by the MA-DANG-LHA-YI-KA-DRO drumming rhythm, either three or seven times.

If this is done slowly, we can recollect all the visualizations and meanings. It is very important to remember the following prayer at this point:

May all sentient beings realize the two bodhichittas.
May all negative karma of sentient beings ripen on me.
May all my happiness be given to all sentient beings in this very lifetime.
In this way may all beings be established in perfect enlightenment.

The real practice of Chöd is unified with the practice of exchange of self for others. If we do not have this pure motivation, the practice will be false.

The descent of nectar from AH marks the end of the preliminaries to the Chöd practice. It is very important to complete the preliminaries correctly.

✍ Actual Practice of Chöd: Gathering the Two Accumulations

T HE ACTUAL PRACTICE of Chöd gathers the two accumulations of merit and wisdom in order to lay the imprints for the two divine bodies of a Buddha: the form body and the truth body. In order to gather the accumulation of merit, we offer our illusory body, and in order to gather the accumulation of wisdom, we meditate on absence of truly existent nature.

GATHERING THE ACCUMULATION OF MERIT BY OFFERING THE ILLUSORY BODY

Offering the illusory body for the accumulation of merit has four parts:

(1) white distribution
(2) red distribution
(3) manifold distribution
(4) giving of Dharma and meditation on taking and giving

The White Distribution

The white distribution is the offering of the refined parts of our bodies by transforming them into nectar. There are two ways of making the white distribution: as a ganachakra offering, or as in the usual Chöd practice. When making the white distribution as a ganachakra offering, we should visualize all of our surroundings as the celestial mandala palace, and all sentient beings around us, even spirits, in the form of the deity, marked with OM AH HUM. The deity could be any, such as Vajrayogini, Heruka,

Yamantaka, or Guhyasamaja, and should be visualized in male-female union.[68] We invoke the wisdom beings and merge with them. The same visualization is done at the beginning of the ganachakra offering section of *Guru Puja*. This visualization is not required for the usual white distribution done in Chöd practice.

To make the white distribution offering, visualize the central channel, straight, having the width of an arrow. The inside is red and the outside is white. At the navel, visualize your mind being present there in the form of a reddish-white drop, half the size of a pea. It is very buoyant, and about to ascend the central channel to the heart of supreme Guru Mother Vajravarahi on the crown of the head. We should not feel separate from this mind drop. Rather, we should really feel that our minds are inside the drop looking upward to the heart of the supreme guru, who is inseparable bliss and emptiness.

Keeping our motive firmly on unifying with the heart of the supreme guru, we should recite PHAT, and visualize in the same way as previously explained for the inner mandala offering. When the former body falls to the ground, it should be seen as huge, fat, white, warm and greasy with fluids and oils. It extends across billions of world systems.

Saying PHAT once more, our mind at the blissful heart of the supreme guru emanates forth as a green action dakini, holding a sharp curved knife. The action dakini makes three circumambulations above the former body, circling in the sky like a vulture. She then lands on the body and immediately proceeds to cut it up with her knife. The first cut is made from the crown to the navel, the next from the heart to the right and left palms, and the last, from the navel to the right and left heels. The skin is then peeled back by the dakini. It is dripping red and covers the whole universe. We should clearly visualize that the ground is completely covered with skin and blood.

To one side arises a tripod of human heads above the peeled skin. The action dakini severs the top of the body's skull from mid-brow between the eyes and hairline, and it cracks apart. This skullcup, or *kapala*, is placed on the tripod and becomes vast. The skullcup seems able to hold an ocean. The dakini fills the skullcup with brains and marrow from the arms, legs, and backbone. Then the dakini pours in the blood, pus, and refined liquids. After these substances are put into the skullcup, the fire of wisdom below the skullcup flares up and melts them. The dakini proceeds to stir the mixture clockwise three times with her knife. The first stirring transforms the mixture into an ocean of medicinal nectar as we recite OM AH HUM. The second stirring transforms the mixture into an ocean of life-prolonging nectar as we recite OM AH HUM. The third stirring transforms the mixture into an ocean of uncontaminated wisdom nectar as we recite OM AH HUM. We should play the damaru slowly each time we recite OM AH HUM. Following the Chöd practice of Panchen Losang Chögyen, we can rest the damaru on the table at this point. This is the brief way of blessing by recitation of OM AH HUM.

The elaborate way of blessing is performed like the inner offering blessing in *Guru Puja*. Under the skullcup, we visualize a wind mandala fanning a fire mandala that blazes up to make the substances melt and boil. Steam rises from the skullcup and spreads to the ten directions, inviting the vajra body, speech, and mind of all the Buddhas in the aspect of OM AH HUM. The OM AH HUM blessing is very important to know because it appears in so many practices, including the *tsog* offering, but its meaning is extremely vast and difficult to visualize.

The three vajra natures of Buddha's body, speech, and mind appear in the aspect of OM, AH, and HUM. As HUM dissolves into the skullcup, it purifies faults of color, smell, and potency. As AH dissolves into the skullcup, it transforms the substances into nectars. As OM dissolves into the skullcup, it makes these nectars inexhaustible. We do not need to visualize the nectars overflowing the skullcup at this point; just imagine that they are inexhaustible.

Usually, in the inner offering, the substances to be transformed are referred to as the five nectars and five meats. According to the Chakrasamvara system, there are five nectars and *four* meats. Some Chakrasamvara systems include human flesh, with the seed syllable BAM, to complete the total of five meats. According to the Yamantaka system, however, there are *four* nectars and five meats. In different aspects of Yamantaka, HUM or BAM is added to generate urine as the fifth nectar. Remember whichever one you use.

In Guhyasamaja it is different again.[69] The four nectars are visualized in either the four cardinal directions or the four intermediate directions, according to the various tantric systems. In the Chöd system we should be practical and use the *Guru Puja* system if we are going to engage in a more extensive inner offering blessing.

It is essential to understand the significance of the syllables OM AH HUM in the blessing of the inner offering. HUM is the seed syllable of Buddha Akshobya, whose nature is the wisdom of dharmadhatu, the vajra mind of all the Buddhas. At the time of the result, when we become Buddhas, we are never separated from this wisdom of dharmadhatu, the wisdom that realizes emptiness directly. This dharmadhatu wisdom purifies all delusion, negativities, and other faults. The wisdom realizing emptiness is so powerful that it can easily purify the substances in the skullcup. That is why HUM is visualized as descending into and purifying the skullcup substances.

AH is the seed syllable of Buddha Amitabha, whose nature is the vajra speech of all the buddhas. "Amitabha" is actually colloquial Sanskrit. The proper name in Sanskrit is "Amita Deva." *Amita* means "undying," or "deathless." *A* is negative, and *mita* means *to die.* The seed syllable AH dissolving into the substances transforms them into nectars of deathless immortality.

OM is the seed syllable of Vairochana, whose nature is the vajra body of all the buddhas. Vairochana represents the pure body of all the countless Buddhas. The seed syllable OM dissolving into the substances makes them inexhaustible in quantity.

All of us have the five aggregates. If these are purified, their nature becomes one with the buddhas. If we purify our physical form, this becomes Buddha Vairochana. In the same way, the feeling aggregate becomes Ratnasambhava, the discrimination aggregate becomes Amitabha, the compositional factor aggregate becomes Amoghasiddhi, and the consciousness aggregate becomes Akshobya.

To summarize, we should think that through the power of these three syllables dissolving, the skullcup substances are transformed into the three nectars—medicinal, life prolonging, and undefiled wisdom nectar. By just tasting this nectar, the sick can be healed, someone dead for up to seven days can be revived, and the wisdom of uncontaminated bliss and emptiness is experienced. "Contaminated" in this context refers to delusion, so all of our present enjoyments are completely contaminated.

Having blessed the inner offering for the white distribution, the actual offering is performed. We visualize many offering dakinis emanating from our own hearts in the form of action dakinis scooping up the offering from the skullcups with their own skullcups. They offer the nectar to the field of merit and assembled guests.

It is very important to know the significance of food and drink offerings and the ways of tasting such offerings. This is important to know whether we are practicing Sutra or Tantra. We know how to eat, how to use cutlery. The cooks and the guests know the purpose of setting out the plates, knives, forks, and so on in a particular way. Likewise, we should be as precise in visualizing the dakinis offering nectars to the field of merit and the guests.

In general, the holy recipients of the white distribution accept the nectar through vajra straws that emanate from their tongues. In particular, we should think of the seven ways of accepting offerings when we are making offerings of nectar transformed into various foods. These seven ways are accepting food by eating, chewing, tasting, licking (pure yogurt, for example), sucking (sugar cane, for example), swallowing (rice porridge, for example), and experiencing. When we set up offerings on an altar, we should imagine that all the offering substances are accepted in one or more of these ways. There are many rituals in Sutra such as Medicine Buddha sadhana and Offerings to the Sixteen Arhats that involve these ways of offering.

What is the correct way to offer nectars? The infinite dakinis emanating from our hearts descend onto the oceanlike surface of the nectar in the skullcup like swans coming to a lake. They take up nectar in their skullcups, which then transforms into fruit, cakes, sugar cane, drinks, and so on. These offerings are made to the assembled beings, who emanate light tubes from their tongues to receive them. They develop great bliss as a result.

We should know the manner in which to make each section of the offering, and the proper attitude to hold towards each type of guest. When making offerings to the gurus, yidams, and the Three Jewels, we should generate great respect and love for them as if for a precious king. When offering to the dharma protectors, we should do so in a manner of making offerings to a friend. When offering to the spirits, we should feel courageous and confident. Feeling powerful, we give to these greedy frustrated spirits. When making offerings to mother sentient beings of the six realms, we should do so with great compassion for their destitute condition and misery. As we make the offering to each of the types of guests, we say OM AH HUM.

The first offering is to the root and lineage gurus. It is very important to know who these are. The root gurus are any gurus from whom you have received teachings. This includes Chöd teachings, mudra gestures, the alphabet, and so on. The lineage gurus are any of your gurus from whom you have not directly received teachings, such as Buddha Vajradhara. Having made offerings of oceans of uncontaminated nectar, we should request in this way:

> Please empower me with your blessings
> That I may understand your stainless liberation!

It is vital to understand why we need to request blessings from the gurus. We need such blessings in order to avoid negative thoughts towards our gurus in regard to actions of body, speech, and mind they may take that are currently beyond our comprehension. If we see the guru as angry, or wrongly criticizing us, or perhaps even beating us, this is due to our mistaken understanding. This is not the guru's fault; it is our fault.

A lama's actions are sometimes difficult to understand. For example, there is a story about Longdöl Lama. When he was very young he was extremely poor and was badly treated. Once he was imprisoned, and while in prison, continually prayed that all his fellow prisoners be released from bad migrations. When he became a realized being he rarely smiled in discourses, and sometimes threatened his disciples with a stick. Once he beat a chant-leader who held a long-life prayer session for him despite having been requested not to.

At this time the abbot of Gomang Monastery died, and one of his monks came to Longdöl Lama to make offerings on behalf of the abbot.

An assistant who came with the monk was the incarnation of the bodhi-sattva Sadaprarudita, "Always Crying."[70] Longdöl Lama was the incarnation of Guru Dharmodgata, whom this bodhisattva had always sought.

Longdöl Lama told his attendant, whose name was Dak, that someone would come to see him the next day, but that he would refuse to grant an interview. The next day, the monk from Gomang came and offered Dak brocade and silver on behalf of their recently deceased abbot for Longdöl Lama. Longdöl Lama said that it was difficult to accept such offerings. With his clairvoyance he had seen where the abbot of Gomang had been reborn: as a frog under a stone in Tenum, Tibet. The lama asked his attendant to buy a hammer and chisel, and together they went to the place the lama had seen. They cracked the stone and found the frog underneath.

At this point Longdöl Lama sent his attendant to Lhasa with the frog and brocade and silver offerings. Following his lama's instructions, the attendant gave the frog and offerings to an old bearded Muslim who, just as the lama had said, was reluctant to accept them. The Muslim ate the frog, except for one leg, which he returned to the attendant for the lama. When he was shown the leg, Longdöl Lama was critical of the attendant, saying that the entire frog should have been eaten. In order to purify this error, the lama made 100,000 small statues of Buddha, recited 100,000 Vajrasattva mantras, and made 100,000 fire-puja offerings.

From this story we can see that we cannot imitate or understand the lama's actions; instead, we should admire the lama's qualities of body, speech, and mind to generate faith. It is for this reason that we request the understanding of our lamas. There is a great danger of developing negative thoughts and experiencing decrease of faith if we have no admiration for our lama. Due to degeneration of the times, faith has decreased and, unlike Tilopa and Marpa, lamas do not beat their disciples now. These days, lamas smile and give presents to their disciples.

The second offering of the white distribution is made to the yidams. We should emanate infinite offering dakinis, as before, who make offerings of garments, food, and drink to the yidams. At the same time, we visualize the dakinis who have made offerings to the gurus returning back in a crowded rush, like the novice monks serving tea or rice in a monastery. Visualize the yidams around the gurus as in the *Guru Puja* field of merit. After having made the offerings in the form of *tormas*, which the yidams accept through light tubes from their mouths, developing uncontaminated bliss, the offering dakinis dissolve back into our hearts. It is very important to visualize this clearly. We then request the yidams to bestow the supreme and common attainments.

"Supreme attainment" refers to buddhahood. "Common" attainments have two divisions: ordinary and extraordinary. The ordinary attainments are those such as curing the sick, or making or stopping rain. The extraordinary attainments are those siddhis achieved on completion of the subtle generation stage. These include levitation, the ability to pass underground, eye-lotion for far-sightedness, great longevity, and good health. Also included amongst the extraordinary attainments is speed-walking, which makes a month's journey possible in one day. There is also the relic pill called "taking the essence," which bestows the youth of a sixteen-year-old. Invisibility is another extraordinary attainment. This is achieved by anointing our eyes with a substance so that others can be seen, but they cannot see us. The siddhi of "deathlessness" is also possible at this stage, whereby we can live more than a thousand years. The practice called "the risen corpse" can bring two siddhis: of the sword and of gold. For this practice we need a corpse and a faithful assistant. A recitation must be done until the eyes of the corpse open and the tongue protrudes. We must then grasp the corpse and hold its tongue with our teeth, biting it off. If this is not done properly, the risen corpse will kill both practitioners. If it is done correctly, the corpse will become gold, and the tongue will become the sword of flight, enabling us to fly anywhere.

Following the offerings to the yidams, we make offerings to the Three Jewels. The previous offering dakinis are visualized returning and dissolving into our hearts, and then infinite dakinis are again emanated from our hearts, making offerings of uncontaminated nectar to the Three Jewels. We request the Three Jewels to free us from the dangers of samsara and nirvana, nirvana referring to the solitary peace of arhatship. If we achieve Hinayana arhatship, we are attached to peace for a long time. Arhatship therefore distances us from the complete liberation of enlightenment for a long time. The request made here is therefore for the attainment of the full liberation of enlightenment.

The fourth offering is to the protectors of Dharma. We make offerings in the same way as before, and request the protectors to assist us in practicing Dharma sincerely, and to help us achieve the four types of yogic activities: pacifying, increasing, controlling, and wrathful actions.

The next offering, the offering to the spirits, is a very important practice because it involves karmic cause and effect. The fully ripened effects of negative actions created in this life may be experienced in the hell realms; as poverty and famine in the human realm; or as weak health or short life in a human body. Behind these many different effects are accompanying spirits that act to ripen these effects.

There are many accidents caused by spirits. For example, causing harm to naga spirits, who hold grudges for a long time, will bring many difficulties in this or future lives. Nagas, in particular, cause mental disorders and disabilities, physical incapacity, and incurable disease. There are, in general, two types of karmic retaliation: revenge and resentment. The karmic retaliation of revenge usually affects possessions. Our material wealth may disappear due to misfortune, or the ill will of others. Our homes may even be taken away. These effects may be due to spirits seeking to return harm we caused them in previous lifetimes.

The karmic retaliation of resentment usually affects the health of a person. The result may be death. Another way of understanding karmic effects is in terms of obligations. We may have a "life obligation" that arises if we have killed in previous lives; then we will have to be killed by that person or persons in the future. On the other hand, we may have karmic obligations not requiring our death. Paying back these karmic debts through pure offerings is very powerful, and pleases those beings. They do not then commit the negative action of retaliating against us. The two types of karmic retaliation were obviously being experienced when the Tibetans were forced to leave Tibet. If we keep moral discipline, nagas cannot harm us, but karmic illnesses caused by nagas cannot be cured by Western medicine.

There was once a Chinese emperor who had two ministers. One of these ministers slandered the other. The slandered minister then killed the other. The dying minister was determined to gain revenge. Dying with such defiled thoughts, he was reborn as a naga. The murderer developed great regret, and was eventually reborn as a monk. As long as this monk kept moral discipline, the naga was unable to harm him. However, the monk once sat on a throne without permission, and this failure of discipline allowed the naga to harm him. Consequently, a wound developed on his knee, and he experienced great pain. Fortunately, a bhikshu who was an emanation of Avalokiteshvara came to help him, and took the monk to a nearby lake. Once at the lake, the bhikshu told the naga to leave the wound, saying that if the monk were to die, the naga would go to the hell realms. Flicking the wound with a white yaktail, the bhikshu succeeded in causing the naga to leave, and the wound fell off into the lake. The monk was then completely cured.

When practicing Chöd we should visualize the spirits around us waiting to retaliate so that we can pacify their attachment to returning harm to us and pacify their resentment of our bodies. The dakinis offer the spirits gifts of gold, minerals, or whatever they wish. After making the offerings, we should pray that the spirits abandon their harmful intentions and attain minds of love. Lastly, we make offerings to the six types of sentient beings. Again the dakinis make offerings of nectar as we recite:

> Giving it to the poor guests, six realms' beings,
> May kindness be returned, may you be freed from pain!

We should strongly visualize all six types of sentient beings in front of us, and that by being given nectar, they are purified into perfect buddhahood.

The Red Distribution

The red distribution is the offering of the remaining flesh, blood, and bones of our former bodies to the spirits, nagas, and other nonhuman beings. It is important to have the correct attitude for this offering; specifically, that we are the host, the invited beings are the guests, and the action dakinis are the cooks for a great banquet. We visualize that the remaining flesh is as vast as countless valleys and mountains, inexhaustible and fresh. Above this, each practitioner visualizes his or her mind in the form of a wisdom dakini inviting all spirits to come to that place and to consume the body. The spirits come immediately from the peak of cyclic existence and from all other realms of cyclic existence down to the hell realms.

It is extremely important to satisfy these spirits. From the moment we are born, we are threatened by eighty thousand different obstacles. It is only our wholesome actions and the dharma protectors that have saved us from harm of spirits so far in this life. It is essential to offer food and other things to spirits to pacify them.

There are many different spirits and obstructions. Spirits may help us if we help them, or retaliate against us if we interfere with them. Obstructions, on the other hand, always interfere with us. They are of two kinds: those that are sentient and those that are not. An example of a nonsentient obstruction is a drought or famine.

In the past there were fewer obstacles caused by spirits. In previous times, many sentient beings attained realizations and buddhahood very quickly. For example, amongst the eighty mahasiddhas, there were many who attained enlightenment in an hour! Nowadays, however, tantric practitioners find it difficult to observe their commitments. Such beings will be reborn as spirits who cannot be destroyed or subdued by mantras like HUM HUM PHAT! Such spirits cannot make spiritual progress quickly to again be able to take a precious human rebirth. Definitely, at present, there are some spirits who have harmful intentions toward practitioners.

Waving her knife in space, the wisdom dakini invites all spirits to come. There are many classifications of spirits to be considered, for example, the three hundred sixty types of "possession" by spirits. According to the White Umbrella system, there is one type of spirit who only harms children. Such a spirit is placated by sweet offerings. One list of spirits is as follows. Spirits of white, reddish, and black colors (these are maras); spirits of variegated color (these are planetary or astrological forces or spirits); spirits of maroon color (these are nagas); cannibal spirits; powerful "king" spirits (tantrikas reborn as spirits); female spirits; landlord or local spirits; and Yama, lord of death.

The distinction between nagas and nyen spirits should also be understood. Nagas are spirits of beings who have practiced generosity but not moral discipline in a previous rebirth. There are many more nagas than human beings. They are wealthy but vindictive and easily affronted. They control water and the oceans. Nyen live in space, not water, and they are similar to nagas.

Another listing of spirits includes devas (gods), nagas, yakshas (wealth deities), gandharvas (celestial musicians), asuras (aggressive demigods), garudas, kinnaras (diminutive spirits, said to be very handsome), mahoragas (big-bellied serpent spirits), manusas (humans), and amanusas (non-humans). This list comes from the text of *Cha Sum*, the Three-Part ritual performed when people are sick.[71] As part of this ritual, tormas are sent out for spirits, and a short recitation is done. Human beings are included in this listing because they can also enter into another being's mind-body continuum.

Another set of spirits includes those in the vast retinue of Indra. This Indra is not the god Indra, but a spirit with a thousand eyes. Guru Padmasambhava extensively explained many of these categories of spirits. He listed internal, external, secret, emanation, and supreme spirits.

In any case, when guests for the red distribution are summoned, we should at least imagine that there are many types of spirits who come in answer to our invitation. Just as a civic reception can be held for many guests who are strangers, so should we imagine Chöd's red distribution. The difference, of course, is that now around us are the spirits of disease and catastrophe, not polite guests. It is vital at this time to recall that all these beings have been our mothers, and to remember their kindness. Do not be afraid of them or angry with them.

In order to summon the guests for the red distribution, we blow the thighbone trumpet three times. The first blowing should be gentle and smooth, and we should think that we are calling the gods and spirits of the three worlds, above, on, and below the earth. The second blowing should also be smooth and gentle, but with a short break in the middle. With it, we imagine that we are calling, "O gods and spirits of the three worlds, please come here!" With the third blowing, we should blow more forcefully, and make two short breaks. At the same time we think, "Gods and spirits of the three worlds, come here! Gather here now!" We should then briefly meditate that our minds, in the form of the wisdom dakini, cannot be harmed, and that we are dedicating our bodies to the objects of our fear, whether animate or inanimate. Another way to describe the red distribution is "pacifying the spirits with bodhichitta."

In the Chöd practice called *Gateway for Those Seeking Liberation,* by Kachen Yeshe Gyaltsen, the spirits, gods and demons are summoned for the red distribution as follows:

> Gather like rainclouds above me!
> Come in a dark red tumultuous storm!
> Spirits of the ten directions!
> Come with weapons! Whistle and moan!
> Be frightening and terrifying!
> Come here right now!

Some spirits do not like the Dharma, and have bad intentions. Thinking this, recite clearly and steadily:

> Come! Come because of our karmic link.
> We have been children and mothers.
> Here is the heap of bones and flesh, the ocean of blood.
> It is a Mount Meru of flesh amidst the ocean.
> These substances are alive, warm, and steaming.
> I have sacrificed my body for your benefit.
> I have given up self-cherishing mind.
> Accept this gift right now, my kind mothers!

We then think that the spirits come in a great rush with much expectation, from all directions, around, above, and below us.

Once the guests have assembled, the wisdom dakini commands them, reminding them that they have been mother and child to each other so they should not fight or compete greedily amongst themselves. Then, without a trace of self-cherishing, encourage the spirits to consume the offering of your former body. You should imagine very strongly that the spirits rend the flesh, break the bones, and drink the blood noisily in their ravenous hunger. Visualizing this scene clearly, do not have any attachment to your body, life force, or merit. We should give to the spirits freely. Finally we tell the guests forcefully:

> Don't leave anything!
> Take with you all that cannot be eaten now!
> Please cook the remains elsewhere and eat it with relish later!
> Don't leave any flesh or blood here!

In this way, practice generosity without miserliness. We warmly and kindly remind the spirits that they have been satisfied, and that henceforth they should be pleasant and helpful to all beings, develop love and compassion, and abandon harmful minds and evil actions.

In general, to make rapid progress in Chöd practice we must eventually go to frightening places and try to see signs of spirits. With pure motivation we should make offerings to them. In this way we can overcome hindrances to developing bodhichitta. We should have no expectation of fame, and no pride thinking that we could gain great power. Certainly we should have no fear of being eaten by evil spirits, because we have already completely given up our bodies. In this respect, the preliminary meditations on motivation and the "four ways of going" are very important.

The Manifold Distribution

The skin that remains after the white and red distributions is cut into many pieces by the wisdom dakini and transformed into whatever the spirits desire for the benefit of all sentient beings. All the skin is cut up and visualized transforming into gold, silver, garments, medicines, fields, mansions, and so on. These fill the whole universe.

We should imagine strongly that all beings receive whatever they wish and are fully contented. This is material generosity. We dedicate and pray that all gods and spirits may obtain their desires. A bodhisattva's prayers may bring quick results. For example, Bodhisattva Akashagarbha, through the power of expressing words of truth, manifested five hundred husbands for five hundred women. As aspirational prayers, those of Akashagarbha, Samantabhadra and Manjushri are very powerful. In a similar way,

Chöd practitioners can make prayers of aspiration on behalf of other sentient beings in the context of this manifold distribution. Whatever they desire, be it an island, a shelter, a protector, or a guru, pray for them to acquire it. Sincere, pure practitioners of Chöd should make very strong prayers at this point.

If we act with virtue, we will definitely experience positive effects. For example, in the time of King Prasenajit, there was a farmer who harvested gold with his crops. The king confiscated the gold and gave the farmer wheat fields in return. Yet even in these new fields, the same harvest of gold was reaped. This occurred because the farmer had once made elaborate offerings. Nowadays, a wholesome action is rare. In order to create merit, we must make offerings. If we concentrate only on offering flowers and fruit, however, this may lead to rebirth as a monkey!

When food was eaten in Tibet, often it was only tsampa. In Tibetan monasteries monks would offer two handfuls of tsampa as a torma[72] to Hariti, the "Wrathful Mother," with the mantra OM HARITE SVAHA, and to her five hundred children with another, longer mantra. This is in remembrance of Hariti's promise to give up human sacrifice and cannibalism if such tormas were daily offered to her and her family.

It is crucial to make offerings to create merit; otherwise, we will be spiritually impoverished and materially poor. King Munindra became the king of four continents and joint ruler of the Land of Thirty-three.[73] Why? Because in a previous life he offered seven grains of rice to Lord Buddha. Four grains fell into Buddha's bowl, one balanced on the rim, and two grains fell to the ground.

At one time there was a couple so poor they only had one piece of clothing between them. They lived in a grass hut, and only one of them could go out at a time. One day they saw people making offerings to Buddha, and greatly admired them. Later, the husband met a bhikshuni, and asked if he could offer their piece of clothing to create merit. Receiving news of this, Buddha dedicated the merit of the offering, and that very day the couple received more clothes. In their next lives they received clothes effortlessly.

There is another story illustrating the power of offering practice. At the time of Buddha in India, there was a poor woodsman who offered his entire wealth, a silver coin in a jar of water, to the Buddha. In his next life he became wealthy and had a child who, from birth, could produce gold coins from his hands. This was a result of his father having offered a silver coin to the Buddha.

Tibetan children used to play various games with sticks and stones, imagining that they were horses and so forth. Such children's play was common in ancient India, and once a child offered dust to the Buddha, visualizing it as food, gold, and jewels. He was short, and, in order to make the offering, had to stand on the back of his friend who was bending over. Buddha kept this dust and asked for it to be used to repair temples and statues. He prophesied that the child who offered the dust would become a powerful king in the future, and that the child helping him would become his minister. This king, the Buddha prophesied, would build millions of stupas. The child later became King Ashoka, who had ten million stupas built in one day. This happened through the power of expressing truth.

When practicing Chöd, we are making very meritorious offerings, but we should regard these offerings as a continuous practice of purification. Begin any offering practice with the seven-limb prayer, and include both actually prepared and mentally envisioned offerings. In general, practitioners need a mandala base to make mandala offerings properly, but we should not regard daily life activities or possessions as more important to us than the Three Jewels. For every offering that we make, we must include dedication prayer. For example, when offering light, we can recite this prayer, offered to the Buddha by a disciple:

> Out of faith I make this offering of light
> To Buddha, Dharma, and Sangha.
> Through the merit, may all sentient beings
> In all lives be endowed with the lamp of wisdom,
> Clearing all darkness of ignorance from their minds!

Never be content thinking you've made enough offerings. Again, try to make your practice of offering a continual practice of purification.

Giving material things to sentient beings with pure motivation is the practice of charity free of clinging or miserliness. Due to our training, we must always be ready to give our bodies, as we have very little materially to give. Giving our bodies purely is more beneficial than giving material things. Even though we still have our bodies when we have finished, if we practice sincerely, the beneficiaries will definitely receive the offering. Similarly, food offerings made on the altar are not visibly taken away by the Buddhas! Offering should be regarded as the cultivation of our own minds in generosity.

Giving of love can be practiced by meditating on love for all sentient beings for even a few minutes. This is very helpful for generating actual love that is unfabricated and spontaneous. Meditating on love for even a few minutes is more beneficial than giving a feast for three hundred people.

If we meditate on love, we will automatically develop compassion. Love is the wish to establish beings in happiness. It is a primary mind devoid of hatred. Compassion is a mind that wishes for beings not to be harmed in any way. It is a secondary mind devoid of anger. It is not the same as love.

In Chöd we practice many different kinds of generosity. If we can engage in this practice of generosity correctly, it is very beneficial to all sentient beings as well as to ourselves. By practicing generosity properly, we can gain the first spiritual ground.

Giving Dharma and Meditating on Taking and Giving

After having practiced the generosity of giving our material body in the previous distributions, we practice the generosity of giving Dharma in order to fully ripen the minds of all beings.

We begin the practice of giving Dharma by recalling that all migrators have been our parents in previous lives. Remembering their beginningless kindness, we determine to return their kindness by teaching them Dharma after having offered them our bodies. The teaching of Dharma is included in two stanzas that represent the wisdom and method aspects of Lord Buddha's teachings. The first stanza is as follows:

> Thus, all compounded things are impermanent.
> Also, all that's deluded is suffering in nature.
> All is just selfless dependent arising.
> Meditating on these, you'll gain peace of nirvana.

These four lines are the "four seals," or summaries, of Dharma. They contain the entire teachings of Dharma. All stages of *lamrim* are contained within these four seals. Reliance on the guru is implicit, though not explicitly mentioned.

Thus, all compounded things are impermanent. There are two types of impermanence: gross and subtle. Gross impermanence can be seen with gross perception; for example, the breaking of a cup or chair, seasonal changes, the passage of the sun from east to west, the death of a realized teacher, and so on. Gross impermanence is easier to understand, because it is obvious to our experience.

The most powerful method to stimulate our Dharma practice is to meditate upon these two types of impermanence. Anything that is produced by causes and conditions will definitely disintegrate. If we have a table made of wood, carpenters and painters may have put great effort into making it, but in the next moment after it has been finished it starts to disintegrate. A human body, for instance, is the result of accumulated moral discipline from previous lives, but it is disintegrating moment by moment from the very instant of birth. No other condition is necessary for this to happen. It happens naturally through the conditions created by birth itself. Our present world system seems to be stable and firm, yet it, too, is in the process of disintegration. This process takes eons until it is destroyed. Any phenomenon that is produced by causes and conditions is impermanent. Contemplating gross impermanence in this way leads us to understand the need for Dharma practice.

Subtle impermanence is not understood simply by hearing the statement, "All products are impermanent," however. Subtle impermanence can be understood only through correct logical reasoning, and not, at first, through direct perception. It is said that subtle impermanence is only realized through signs or indications. Let us consider an "indestructible" diamond. It is thought to be very strong and stable, yet it is actually in a constant state of change, as the present moment passes and the future moment arises. We do not perceive this change. If we see that causes and conditions are impermanent, we can understand that the phenomena they produce are also necessarily impermanent. All five sense-objects—form, sound, smell, taste, and touch—and the five aggregates—form, feeling, recognition, karmic formations, and consciousness—are "compound phenomena," because they are produced through the power of causes and conditions. If something is a product it must disintegrate every moment without pause. We do not at present understand this constant momentary change.

Even if we do not understand subtle impermanence, we must understand gross impermanence. Everyone can understand the process of gross impermanence, the visible erosion or disintegration of produced phenomena. Wherever we look we can see gross impermanence clearly and directly. For example, today, this discourse is taking place. After several hours we will enjoy food, perhaps some sunshine, then another discourse. This process of change is obvious. What is vital to realize is that change also affects our bodies and possessions. Both will definitely disintegrate. The bodies and possessions of others also disintegrate and therefore will not help us in any way.

The reason impermanence is the subject of the first of the four seals is that followers of Buddha must become determined to practice Dharma continuously. This is best achieved through mindfulness of impermanence and death. Dharma practitioners can definitely fall to unfortunate rebirth if they are not mindful of death and impermanence.

As he was passing away, Buddha greatly stressed the need to keep impermanence in mind at all times. At his parinirvana at Kushinagar, Buddha told the sangha to approach him in order to look at the precious and rare body of a Tathagata. In his last pronouncement he said:

> Of all footprints, that of the elephant is deepest.
> Of all awarenesses, that of impermanence
> Makes the deepest impression on the mind.
> So, bhikshus, remember death and impermanence!

Mindfulness of death and impermanence is the gateway to practice, the practice itself, and the realization of practice. In *lamrim* teachings the faults of not remembering death are listed as six: (1) we don't remember to practice Dharma; (2) we do not practice Dharma; (3) if we do practice Dharma, it is not pure practice; (4) there is no sincere Dharma practice; (5) negativities are continually committed; and (6) we die with regret.

If we are not mindful of death and impermanence, our practice will become mere intellectual curiosity, or it will be motivated by mundane concerns such as fame, pride, or even just food and clothing. In addition, our Dharma practice will become sporadic even if it *is* practiced purely, and negativities of body, speech, and mind will still be committed as a consequence. The result of this is that we will die with regret, remembering our negative actions and fearing the approaching bardo state and rebirth. We may become like Ngödrub Chödak, whose life and death is used as an example in the texts. When he was alive he was like a wise adviser to many people who sought his help. But as he was dying he clutched at his chest with his hands, lamenting his negative actions, and he died with great regret.

Due to forgetting death and impermanence, competitiveness, pride, jealousy, and hostility may develop amongst people. Even within communities of tantric practitioners, discontent, aggression, and abuse may occur. This will result in unfortunate rebirths because one of the Tantric vows has been transgressed. Dharma communities need agreement based on compromise. Slander should not be committed. Atisha said that a certain geshe named Gyapa should have died before causing dissension amongst the sangha.

Once a monastery in Tibet experienced dissent and argument among the monks. This disturbance prevented the lama from receiving his visions of Tara and Chenrezig and from receiving teachings from holy statues. In order to purify these negativities the lama did 100,000 Vajrasattva mantras, 100,000 Vajradaka fire offerings, and made 100,000 tsa-tsas of Buddha. Through such stories we learn the way to purify actions. Harmful actions are invariably committed if we don't remember death and impermanence. We should strive to avoid all negative actions, even the slightest.

Beginners should always begin their practice of Dharma with mindfulness of death and impermanence. If we are teaching Dharma, the first discourse should also be on this point. As Buddha said, "Meeting ends in parting." At the moment we are listening to teachings; yet very soon we shall disperse to different places and to different rebirths. Inevitably families separate. Children cannot live with their parents forever. This type of impermanence should always be remembered.

While reciting these teachings of Buddha, we should think with certainty that the assembled, satiated, and calmed spirits and gods around us are clearly understanding and learning. We imagine that these poor spirits are pleased and benefited by our recitation. Their minds become contented and happier as a result of hearing Buddha's teachings.

Also, all that's deluded is suffering in nature. Another way of expressing this is "All contaminated things are miserable." It is difficult to understand profound Dharma teachings. "Contamination" here means that which is deluded or deluding. On this point it is helpful to look at the very good Vaibhashika[74] presentation of contaminated delusions. There are six root delusions—desirous attachment, anger, ignorance, wrong views, deluded doubts, and the view of the transitory collection[75]—and twenty secondary delusions that derive from these. Anything produced by delusions is contaminated, yet that is all that we have at present. Understanding this, we must develop renunciation, an intention to get free of this contamination. Recognizing that with delusion there is nothing we presently experience that is not of the nature of suffering, we also visualize the assembled guests receiving the teaching. The point to emphasize here is that as long as we have taken a body due to karma, we will definitely experience suffering.

All is just selfless dependent arising. It is by meditating on phenomena being selfless, nontruly existent because of being dependent arisings, that suffering ends. This is because there is no longer compulsive grasping at phenomenal appearances as inherently existent. The delusions cease due to their roots—self-cherishing and self-grasping—having been cut.

Meditating on these, you'll gain peace of nirvana. Nirvana is freedom from suffering because all "contamination" has ceased. In nirvana, the state beyond sorrow, not even the *word* "misery" exists. One no longer experiences the sufferings of cyclic existence, and there is no regression from that state of peace.

Having recited this stanza of the four seals of Dharma, we should imagine that all beings directly realize the truth of emptiness and begin to practice the six perfections.

The next stanza in the sadhana deals with the method aspect of Buddha's teachings:

> Commit not the slightest harmful nonvirtue.
> Persevere in performing perfect virtue.
> As for your mind, thoroughly subdue it.
> Strive to practice this, the teaching of Buddha!

In this way, the spirits are taught not to commit negativities, to accumulate virtue, to control their minds, and to adhere to Buddha's words. In the original form as Buddha taught it, the fourth line is "This is the teaching of Buddha," rather than, "Strive to practice this, the teaching of Buddha." The exhortation to practice was inserted here in order to facilitate the poetry of the sadhana.

In order to attain nirvana or any superior paths of the Three Vehicles, we must realize emptiness directly. It is not sufficient, however, just to gain "liberation"; we need "higher liberation." For this attainment, both method and wisdom practices are required. On its own, wisdom realizing emptiness is not enough. It is like chopping down a tree. This requires wisdom—which is like an axe—and method—the strength and ability to wield it. If all aspects of method and wisdom are strong, higher liberation can easily be attained. Training in higher wisdom is like sharpening the axe. Methods of meditative concentration, like a steady hand, and moral discipline, like a suitably able body, are required as well.

Concentration can only be attained with moral discipline. Many non-Buddhists have gained the concentration of "tranquil abiding" or shamata, but they have not achieved "superior seeing" or insight realizing emptiness. It is very important to distinguish between Buddhist and non-Buddhist paths. Buddhist paths do not require entry into the "actual concentrations"; reaching the stage of "preparation for the actual concentration"[76] is sufficient as a basis for developing insight. Non-Buddhists, however, spend great periods of time in these concentrative states, for example, at the peak of cyclic existence, thinking they have attained liberation. After their karma has ripened, they necessarily descend to lower rebirths, possibly with the very negative thought to abandon their search for liberation, their death indicating to them that what they had previously taken to be liberation was not liberation in reality.

In order to understand spiritual paths we should receive teachings from our lamas on "grounds and paths." There it is explained how Buddhists practicing supramundane paths will not descend to lower rebirth even though they do not achieve the peak of cyclic existence. It is important to study this subject with qualified teachers. While respected geshes reside at Dharma centers, they should put their knowledge to use for their students. If they do not, it is better that they remain at their own monasteries!

Buddhist practitioners can sometimes be hindered by "Ishvara" lords who control others' emanations. The Five Arrows of Ishvara each have the power to afflict a practitioner's mind with a different delusion, but they cannot prevent the attainment of higher liberation if we make appropriate effort.

When we are reciting this stanza of four lines, we should think that the spirits around us have heard the teaching and have understood. Before public discourses, Buddha proclaimed this teaching to his disciples and his audience.

After having completed the practice of recitation of the four seals with the visualization previously described, generate the "superior intention" with immaculate love, taking responsibility to do all that is necessary for the liberation of beings. On examination, it will be found that only fully enlightened beings can benefit others completely. Therefore, with the determination to become a fully realized Buddha for the sake of all sentient beings, we next engage in the practice of taking and giving.

Practice of taking and giving begins with the taking of others' miseries from them. Otherwise beings cannot be made happy by giving. With pure motivation we take the miseries and the two obscurations of others into our bodies through the left nostril in the form of black light, poisons, weapons, spiders, thunderclouds, and so forth. These forms represent all evil, all negative actions, the sufferings specific to all beings of the six realms, and the delusions of all mother sentient beings. As these forms and the black light dissolve at our hearts, we think that they dissolve into our own self-cherishing minds, which then disappears.

We then begin the practice of giving our bodies, our wealth, and our virtues to others. All our wholesome actions of the past, present, and future, our realizations and virtuous Dharma activities of listening, contemplating, meditating, and keeping our vows, all these are transformed into pure white light at our hearts. This white light emanates from the right nostril and touches the hearts of the visualized field of merit. All the realizations and cessations of the holy beings merge with the white light, which then enters the right nostril of all mother sentient beings and blissfully melts into their hearts, blessing and empowering them. We should think of our bodies as wish-fulfilling jewels that grant the wishes of all mother sentient beings throughout space. It is most important to feel that mother sentient beings, especially the devas and spirits around us, are all freed from their sufferings through realizing emptiness, and that they have become tremendously happy.

There are different categories of emptiness, but all can be included within two categories: emptiness of the "I" or person, and emptiness of phenomena other than the person. First we should meditate on emptiness of "I." We should try to find a truly existent "I," and then progress to attempting to find a truly existent object or phenomenon other than the person. The basis of emptiness can be switched from object to object in the latter case. Emptiness is the same for all persons and all objects.

When we do the taking and giving (*tonglen*) practice, we should imagine that all sentient beings have attained realization of the different types of emptiness within their continuums. According to Mahayana, emptiness can be classified in two, four, sixteen, or twenty "emptinesses." Examples are the emptiness of the beginningless (meaning the emptiness of samsara) and the emptiness of emptiness. The only difference is the "basis." Emptiness itself is not separate or different. We study the different types of emptiness in order to deepen our understanding. It is very important to study *lamrim,* and to increase the foundations of our Dharma knowledge and practice. In order to comprehend emptiness, a "hidden object,"[77] we should make every effort to study and meditate upon the Perfection of Wisdom texts.

Bodhisattvas need to meditate on both bodhichitta and emptiness. Bodhichitta should be the pillar of our practice. Meditation on emptiness is the way to progress on the five paths and the ten grounds. Anyone meditating on tranquil abiding—and this is a practice common to both Buddhists and non-Buddhists—needs to be aware of what is referred to as suppleness,[78] otherwise I'm not sure what they could be meditating upon!

When we visualize the field of merit in front of us, we should remember the one hundred seventy-three good qualities of the Buddha as listed in the Seventy Topics,[79] and think very strongly that the objects in the field of merit have all of these. It is these good qualities that we visualize transforming into light and emanating forth to bless and empower all mother sentient beings. This practice brings many benefits and plants the seeds of obtaining these good qualities. It is therefore very important to study the good qualities of the body, speech, and mind of the holy realized beings. These are explained extensively in the Seventy Topics and the *Abhisamayalamkara*. Through the power of receiving these realizations and cessations, all mother sentient beings become buddhas. Their bodies attain the thirty-two major marks and eighty secondary signs of a buddha's body, and their minds become dharmakaya.

Once all mother sentient beings have been ripened and liberated through the giving of Dharma and the practice of taking and giving, they can all depart to their own places, whether in the ground, the water, the mountains, the valleys, or in space. We should think that all the gods, demons, and spirits depart to their own abodes maintaining calm, beneficial minds. However, if we are engaged in the wandering Chöd retreat practice, moving from one place to another, we should not request them to depart, because we need them to remain around us.

GATHERING THE ACCUMULATION OF WISDOM THROUGH MEDITATION ON EMPTINESS

Following completion of the accumulation of merit is the accumulation of wisdom, the method for achieving the truth body, or dharmakaya:

> PHAT
> Giving's three spheres are just labeled names and sounds,
> And exist, not even an atom, from their side.
> Though all living and inanimate things appear to
> Truly exist, they're empty, like illusions.

As indicated in the sadhana, we meditate upon the non-inherent existence of the three spheres of giving.

The Three Spheres of Giving

We must realize that "giving" is merely imputed by name or label. The "substance given" is merely imputed by name, the "giver" is merely imputed by name, and the "recipient" is merely imputed by name. The "giver" is merely labeled in dependence upon his or her collection of aggregates. If things existed inherently, giving would be impossible. It is also very important to meditate carefully upon the three spheres of ethical discipline, patience, effort, and so on. As an introduction to emptiness meditation in Chöd practice, we will first examine the three spheres of giving more thoroughly.

The accumulation of wisdom is the way to make rapid spiritual progress. In Chöd practice we perceive the offering of our illusory bodies to be a practice of charity merely labeled as such by ourselves, with no true existence from its own side. Extending this perception, all phenomena are seen to be nontruly existent, like dreams. It is especially in the practice of Chöd that we find it easy to see that the self who gives, the object given, and the recipient are all three empty of inherent existence.

Usually the three spheres of subject, action, and object appear to be truly existent, and this appearance is apprehended as true. To eliminate this misapprehension we must first apply the exalted wisdom of emptiness. It is very important to be familiar with this wisdom in our daily life because then, when we are practicing Chöd, we can easily recollect this understanding.

Normally we must engage in a great deal of analysis to discover the non-true existence of self. We must directly recognize its dependently arising nature. If we understand this properly, no misapprehension of true existence will arise. If the practice of giving were to be truly existent from its own side it would not depend upon a giver, gift, or a recipient. A giver does not exist without a gift and a recipient. In the same way, an object is not recognized as a gift in the absence of a giver or a recipient. Recipients cannot exist from their own side either without a giver or an act of giving. This is the real understanding of emptiness.

We must apply the same method in order to understand that all phenomena are nontruly existent. For example, let us consider "permanence." Permanence depends upon its opposite, "impermanence." When we assert that something is impermanent, the term "permanent" also arises automatically. "Impermanence" exists by virtue of exclusion of "permanence," and vice versa.[80] This relativism extends to other aspects of phenomena as well; "big" implies "small," "long" implies "short," "this mountain" implies "that mountain." If what these terms referred to existed from their own sides, they would be permanent, independent, and indestructible.

It is due to permanence that we can apply the label "permanent," but if we seek the permanence of an object as something existing from its own side, we discover something inexpressible. If we take three sticks and place them together in a certain way, they will all stand up. If each of the sticks could stand under its own power, it would remain standing even if the others were removed, but they cannot. In this way we must understand dependent arising precisely.

Another way of thinking about it is to consider clothing. Only when cloth is of the correct color, shape, and so forth is it labeled "clothing." Or think of a clock. Whenever we see a clock, we label it a clock, but if we were to separate the component pieces, then the "clock" would cease to exist, because no basis of imputation would remain. In actuality there was no truly existent clock in the first place—only the causes and conditions fit to be labeled a "clock."

The three spheres of giving exist only in terms of dependent relationship. A gift implies both a giver and a recipient. These are mutually supporting elements. Interdependent, they do not exist from their own sides. Without a basis of imputation nothing could be imputed—for example, this building is merely imputed by thought. The three spheres *do* exist, but only conventionally, as imputations. They do not exist from their own sides.

At the moment we may feel that spirits exist from their own sides. This causes fear to develop, but it is the result of a misapprehension. If we meditate on this feeling of inherently existent spirits and inherently existent fear with the same kind of analysis as applied to the three spheres of giving, we will realize the emptiness of the spirits. This emptiness is a

simple, nonaffirming negation. By refuting the seeming inherent existence of gods and spirits, we come to understand how gods and spirits
have been merely imputed by our thoughts. In this way we should destroy
all grasping at spirits as being inherently existent. Absence of truly existent fear and ourselves as truly existent experiencers of fear are realized
at the same time. If we understand emptiness precisely, we will practically
go unconscious at this point.

In general, there are three ways of meditating on emptiness in Chöd
practice. These will be considered later, after a brief explanation of emptiness itself. Many people talk about emptiness, but few have a precise understanding of it. We need a precise understanding for our meditation on
emptiness to be faultless.

When realizing emptiness, we may feel that we are not seeing conventional appearances and that we are falling to a nihilistic position. If we feel
this, we should make sure we are not falling to that extreme, but at the
same time check to see that we are not affirming the reality of conventional appearances, either. We should analyze carefully—is the sense of an
independent "I" one with any of the aggregates? Understanding that neither conventional appearances nor annihilation is real, we realize spacelike emptiness. An instance of the dawning of such realization is that of
a Chöd practitioner who, when he searched for the independent "I," realized that such an "I" existed neither as one with, nor separate from, the
aggregates. As a consequence, he felt himself lifted up into space and
dropped onto the ground! Another example is that of Khedrub Losang
Gyatso, a very humble realized being. Once, when checking for the inherently existent "I" during a discourse on Madhyamika by Je Tsongkhapa,
he experienced fear, and compulsively pulled down his upper robe. Seeing this with his clairvoyance, Je Tsongkhapa expressed his pleasure at
Khedrub Losang Gyatso's reaction. Those who have good imprints for
emptiness from previous lifetimes feel joy when realizing emptiness.
Those without such good imprints develop fear of emptiness, and, as a
consequence, do not realize emptiness as quickly.

In general, there are two kinds of self-grasping, and two lines of reasoning, or "signs," of emptiness. The two kinds of self-grasping are grasp-

ing at a self of persons and grasping at a self of phenomena other than persons. The two ways of realizing the emptiness of persons and other phenomena are the "king of reasoning"—dependent origination, for those of sharp intelligence—and "the logical reasons"—absence of singularity and plurality.

The Logical Reasons

First, we will examine the sign of emptiness termed "the logical reasons." In order to understand this sign of emptiness we must know four essential points. These are

(1) the essential point of ascertaining the object of negation
(2) the essential point of ascertaining pervasion
(3) the essential point of the absence of singularity
(4) the essential point of the absence of plurality

If things exist, they must be one or many, singular or multiple. If they are neither of these, they do not exist. So, if something is an existent phenomenon, it must be either the same as, or different from, any other existent phenomenon.

The Essential Point of Ascertaining the Object of Negation

In order to meditate on our own selflessness, we must identify the proper object of negation. Without identifying the object of negation, meditation on emptiness is like shooting an arrow without knowing where the target is. We must first understand and get the feeling of how the sense of an independent "I" arises.

All of our actions develop under the influence of grasping at an independent "I." Out of self-cherishing, or cherishing others without moral discipline, or both, we commit negativity due to self-grasping ignorance. Meritorious actions that lead to higher samsaric rebirths are also rooted in self-grasping. That is why they cannot free us from cyclic existence. "Unmoving actions" that cause rebirth in the form or formless realms are still influenced by the conception of an independent "I." Examples of these "unmoving actions" are meditations on tranquil abiding, and the actual concentrations. It is easier to free ourselves from the desire realm than it is to free ourselves from the form or formless realms.

At present, the independent, inherently existent "I" wants happiness and not suffering; it wants liberation and highest enlightenment. We must discover the actual mode of existence of this "I." At the moment we are totally under the influence of self-grasping mind, and we must escape from it by seeing the true nature of self.

What does it mean to say that we feel the "I" to be "inherently existent," a term synonymous with "existing from its own side," or "existing objectively"? At the moment, we feel that the "I" exists without the need for a label or a sound; it seems to exist under its own power. With investigation, we should be able to identify this sense of an inherently existent "I." Normally it is difficult to recognize, but adverse conditions can bring up the sense of a concrete, independent "I" very easily. When we are angry at being wrongly accused, for example, it is easier to "catch" the independent "I" with our alertness. What do we do then?

We should not immediately refute this "I." Just as an archer watches the target carefully and takes aim to shoot, we should get the independent "I" to appear clearly, and only then directly refute it. It is very important to make prayers to the merit field for the ability to identify this "I" correctly and clearly; otherwise it is difficult to find the correct object of negation.

There are many ways in which we cling to the "I" as inherently existent. We may cling to the aggregate of form or to the aggregate of consciousness as being the inherently existent "I." If we were to feel ourselves about to fall from a high cliff, we would grasp at the aggregate of form, the body, as the "I" that is about to fall. If we recall our negative actions and consider that we might fall to lower rebirths, we grasp at the aggregate of consciousness as the inherently existent "I." More importantly for our purposes, if we are praised or blamed, our bodies and minds seem wholly full of "I." This is the easiest, most effective way to recognize the object of negation.

It is important not to negate the sense of an inherently existent "I" immediately. We habitually believe that it really exists in the way it appears. Until we realize emptiness, we cannot differentiate between the existent and the nonexistent "I." At present, the independent "I" is so powerful that it seems to develop on its own, not arising from other causal conditions. It seems to control us.

The Essential Point of Ascertaining Pervasion

We must realize that if such an independent "I" existed, it would have to be one with, or separate from, the five aggregates. It is very important to remember this pervasion: if a phenomenon is not "the same as" or "different from" another existent phenomenon, it must not exist.[81]

The Essential Point of Absence of Singularity

If we consider the "I" to be one with the five aggregates, many absurd conclusions follow. There would have to be five different independent "I"s. Not only this, but parts of the form aggregate such as arms and legs would have to be the "I" also, and would remain so even if they were removed from the other parts of the form aggregate. Through such an examination we discover that the independent "I" is not one with the five aggregates, and we conclude that there is an absence of true singularity. The only remaining conclusion is that the independent "I" must be different or separate from the aggregates.

The Essential Point of Absence of Plurality

Is this independent "I" separate from the aggregates? Is the "I" separate from the aggregates in the way that elephants can be distinguished from other animals? Is there an independent "I" really separate from the form aggregate or any of the other aggregates? By checking we will discover that there is no "I" separate from the five aggregates. At this point we should feel that the "I" is lost! This is the correct way to realize emptiness. The initial realization is critical, so we should make requests to the objects of refuge, perform prostrations, accumulate merit, and purify negativities in order to have this experience.

When we are realizing emptiness, this is a simple, or "nonaffirming," negation. It is realized by way of explicitly refuting inherent existence, without anything else being implied or affirmed. After Je Tsongkhapa passed away, there was some debate on this point among meditators. In order to clarify this, Dulnagpa Palden Lama, the lama who composed *Ganden Lhagyema,*[82] and who had achieved the path of seeing, was asked for his judgment. He said that if we experience fear that the "I" is lost, emptiness is realized. We should then continue to meditate on emptiness of inherent existence to deepen the realization.

In Chöd practice, it is easier to find and identify the object to be negated. When practicing Chöd, we do so alone and at night, sometimes in frightful places such as graveyards, in order to develop fear. Fear may arise due to noises, shapes, anxieties, or just the darkness. When this fear arises, the inherently existent "I," the object of negation, is seen clearly. At this point we should eject our consciousness into space, thinking that our minds merge with space as the wisdom dakini. When we are sacrificing our former bodies to the spirits, there is no reason to be afraid. We have no body to be attached to, because we have already given it up. Our minds cannot be harmed because we have mixed them with space. Without these two, there can be no self-grasping. In this way we come to actually understand emptiness. If we feel that the "I" is "lost" for the remainder of the practice, we are realizing emptiness.

When emptiness is realized, we can experience no harm or violent appearances. It is the fear of harm and violent appearances that causes the independent "I" to arise. It is then lost when examined, and consciousness is ejected into space. At this point, we may go unconscious with fear and the mixing of awareness with space. If this happens, strongly feel that the independent "I" has been destroyed. Through fear and the merging of mind with space, we come to understand the nature of the nominal, conventionally existent "I," as well as the absence of inherently existent "I." Chöd is a special method to experience the nonexistence of an inherently existent "I."

In the same way, by precisely recognizing the object of negation, we understand the non-inherent existence of other phenomena. Realizing emptiness of self, we transcend all fear. We can absorb all appearances around us into light. As the text says, "living and inanimate things are empty, like illusions." This means that all appearances of this world system, and the living beings therein, are empty of inherent existence. Until we reach the path of seeing, we experience these illusory appearances as "real." Absorbing all these appearances into light, we meditate on the three spheres'—giver, gift and receivers'—emptiness of inherent existence. Once all appearances are completely absorbed into our hearts as light, we should meditate on emptiness—conceptually, at first.

In order to meditate on emptiness conceptually, we need to know how to differentiate between the four objects of conceptual thought. These are the apprehended object, the engaged object, the conceived object and the appearing object. Of these four objects of conceptual thought, the appearing object, in particular, must be thoroughly understood. This type of object is, for example, the recollection of things in our rooms while we are in the meditation hall, the generic images we remember. These objects of conceptual thought are known in many ways. Let us consider a plate, for example. If we recall a plate we have used, this is a generic image of a plate. Someone else might know of the existence of plates only through having heard the name "plate," a "sound generality," rather than through recollection of an object. The objects that appear to conceptual thought are therefore the type of mind referred to as a "subsequent cognition," because they are developed subsequent to a direct perception.

The engaged object is that which is understood or apprehended. In the case of blue being apprehended conceptually, by means of thought, the engaged object is the color blue. The apprehended object refers to the direct perception that is remembered.

When the conceived object of thought appears to the mind, it is grasped as being identical with that which was previously perceived; for example, a plate that was seen, before it is seen again. The conceptual mind conceives its appearing object, the generic image, to be of one nature with the previously perceived object. But the object which appears to thought is *not* the actual object. For instance, the plate that appears to our minds may appear to us even if it no longer exists, as when a dog breaks a plate in the other room while we are still remembering it. What is erroneous is the belief that the conceived object of conceptual thought is the actual object itself. In actuality, the engaged object of conceptual thought is not the thing itself, either: it is the memory of a direct perception. Nonconceptual sense consciousness does not have a conceived object, because whatever appears to *it* is perceived directly, without the need for any conceptual clarification as to what the object is. It is this process of clarification, and thus conceptualization, that must be thoroughly understood in examining the four objects of conceptual thought.

We must study Collected Topics and Mind and Cognition[83] on an experiential level; otherwise it is a mere intellectual curiosity. We must seek to internalize it in a practical way. Try to deepen your study by penetrating the profundity of the teachings. It is not enough to understand them superficially. We must work with them every day, at every moment.

Similarly, when practicing Chöd we must continually deepen our understanding of emptiness by contemplating how everything is non-inherently existent. At the point when all appearances melt into light and dissolve into your heart, feel that you are seeing emptiness. This emptiness is the appearing object of your conceptual understanding. Think, "this emptiness," the appearing object, "does not exist from its own side." That is the conceived object. In that way, we understand emptiness, not through direct perception but conceptually, at first. By improving our conceptual understanding, focusing without distraction upon our generic image of emptiness, we come to realize emptiness directly. We must clearly distinguish between the appearing object—empty space—and the conceived object—the thought that it does not inherently exist—in order to meditate properly on emptiness.

What is the particular mode of cognition being used in this type of conceptual meditation on emptiness? In general, there are various ways of knowing something. Is it direct perception? No, obviously not. Is it inference? That is not the case, either. Is it the type of awareness to which something appears, yet is not ascertained? No, because emptiness has not yet appeared to our minds directly. Another mode of awareness is that of doubt, but such a mind could not meditate on emptiness, due to being uncertain of its object, and lacking any fixed concentration. Neither is Chöd meditation on emptiness a "recollection" or "subsequent cognition." By checking our knowledge of mind and cognition, with experience we will conclude that the meditation on emptiness in Chöd is by way of correct belief. We must put the teachings to use, not just study them as objects of observation, like geography.

There are various types of correct beliefs. For example, there is correct belief based on reasoning which has been established, and there is correct belief based on reasoning which has not been established. In order to clarify these, let us consider the way that we meditate on emptiness as explained so far. If we recollect the teachings on emptiness of the three spheres of giving, this is meditation on emptiness by way of a "sound generality." If, however, we understand what "mere imputation by thought" means, this is meditation on emptiness through a generic image. If we were to meditate on emptiness believing that the emptiness of the three spheres of giving is established by reason of their not being one or separate, we would be meditating on emptiness with correct belief based on reasoning which has not been established. This is because it is the wrong kind of reasoning to apply in this case. The correct reasoning for emptiness of the three spheres is the reasoning of dependent relationship. Until we achieve a direct perception of emptiness, the mind of correct belief is very unstable, like pounding a stake or tent peg into wet ground. It is very important to master the four essential points in order to thoroughly negate the object to be eliminated. If we can do this successfully, we will attain a direct perception of emptiness. At that point, we are capable of meditating on emptiness with correct belief based on reasoning that has been established, induced by our direct perception.

Once we have meditated on emptiness analytically, we should follow this with placement meditation: spacelike meditative equipoise on emptiness. When we rise from this equipoise into what is called our "subsequent attainment" Chöd practice, this should not disrupt our spacelike meditative equipoise, but rather should complement it, as we view all things as illusions, like waves stirred up on the surface of a deep, quiet ocean. All conventional appearances should be perceived as illusions arising from emptiness in this way.

There are several ways of meditating. Meditation does not always require cross-legged sitting posture. We can meditate on emptiness while our body is moving; absolute stillness of the body is not necessary. It is not the body that meditates, but the mind. We can meditate while walking or even lying down. When we receive instruction on generation stage practices of Highest Yoga Tantra, we learn about the yogas of rising, eating, and sleeping. These yogas are meditation, also. Machig Labdrön told her disciples that such yogas existed, but that no one knew how to do them properly. The practices of circumambulation, prostration, and pilgrimage should be done as meditations also. In the *Flower Ornament Sutra*[84] Buddha said, to paraphrase, "When entering a doorway, regard it as entering the gateway to liberation. When closing a door, think of it as closing the door to samsara. When sitting down, regard it as escaping from samsara; when standing up, regard it as having attained liberation." We should be mindful of what is actually happening in a formal meditation session. This particular sutra lists many ways of meditating.

For Chöd practitioners, all of our actions are meditations. Just as soldiers in war should be inseparable from their weapons, in a similar way, Chöd practitioners should be inseparable from method—bodhichitta, the mind of enlightenment—and wisdom—the understanding of emptiness. Chöd practitioners are warriors, too. They are battling self-cherishing and self-grasping. They are not fighting spirits. Towards spirits we should always cultivate love and compassion.

While practicing Chöd it is important to gather the two accumulations of merit and wisdom. We must complete the accumulation of wisdom by realizing emptiness in order to sever the conceptual self-grasping that is the very root of cyclic existence. If we lack wisdom at any time during the practice of Chöd, we are like soldiers who have dropped our weapons on the field of battle. From refuge practice onwards, we should always keep emptiness in mind. Perceiving the objects of refuge as empty of inherent existence, we absorb them into our hearts. Then we meditate on emptiness. This is the very important practice of ultimate guru yoga, also. By being mindful of emptiness in the refuge practice, all our practice becomes deep and powerful.

Whatever practice we do, we should keep bodhichitta and wisdom together. There is no other way to develop tantric realizations, either. Union of bliss and emptiness is not explicitly revealed in Chöd, so it cannot be classified as tantra, but Chöd practice must involve the union of bodhichitta and emptiness at all times. Some people claim that Chöd is not sutra practice because it involves radiating light and other visualizations, and that it is not generation stage practice of secret mantra, either, because no deity is generated. They say it is only a "Tibetan Dharma," an invalid teaching created by Tibetans. Yet many Indian pandits practiced Chöd, despite this criticism, and discovered it to be especially effective in subduing their self-cherishing and self-grasping. We are exceptionally fortunate to be able to practice Chöd.

It is said that if we abandon bodhichitta and the wisdom that cuts the root of samsara, other practices cannot help us destroy self-cherishing and self-grasping. We should never neglect cultivating wisdom and compassion.

It is important that we meditate on emptiness with correct awareness of the successive stages of development of tranquil abiding, or *shamata*. In particular, we must know what mental sinking is, how it causes dullness, erodes the memory, and stops discriminating wisdom from arising. Je Tsongkhapa stressed the need to avoid subtle mental sinking, and presented, as did Bhavaviveka, the methods for accomplishing tranquil abiding. In general, we should follow the path of the past, present, and future buddhas. In particular, we must meditate on *lamrim* thoroughly and continuously. In former lives we have all attained siddhis and had visions of deities, yet we still remain bound in cyclic existence. Devas, with all their abilities, are still subject to rebirth. Only our own efforts and realizations can free us.

Three Methods for Meditation on Emptiness in Chöd Practice

According to Chöd, there are three ways we can meditate on emptiness: (1) without mental facility, (2) through searching the superstitions, and (3) through analytical investigation.

Meditation on Emptiness Without Mental Facility

The first type of meditation on emptiness is easiest for beginners. After reciting the stanza on emptiness of the three spheres of giving, we conclude that all phenomena do not exist from their own sides, that they are like illusions. No fear can arise because the body has been sacrificed, and there remains no attachment to the aggregates. Our consciousness has been dissolved into space. So who is it that cares about that form on the ground? Having dissolved our minds in space we should become like unconscious corpses. We meditate on emptiness with tranquil abiding, free from mental sinking and excitement. An object of tranquil abiding meditation must be something with which we have already become familiar. In this meditation, the mind must realize its own nontrue existence and, therefore, the nontrue existence of all illusory appearances. This method accords with the Mahamudra system. Intelligent practitioners practice this meditation as a means to develop the correct view of emptiness.

Meditation on Emptiness by Searching the Superstitions

When we are meditating in a haunted graveyard, or even in our rooms, frightening external and internal appearances may arise during Chöd practice. If this happens, check the two "superstitions"—the external, frightening appearance, and the internal appearance of the inherently existent "I" that is frightened. Do they exist from their own sides? With determination, check for the "I" that experiences fear, whether of a sight or a sound. Recalling that our purpose is to compassionately sacrifice ourselves to the spirits, and remembering emptiness of the three spheres of giving, we mix our minds with space and visualize the spirits consuming our bodies as well as our sense of inherently existent self. After the spirits have eaten the body, again investigate the two superstitions. It is by checking for the independent "I" that we come to realize emptiness.

Meditation on Emptiness with Analytical Meditation

The usual way to meditate on emptiness is to investigate self-grasping. When frightening appearances arise, the self feels threatened and appears very powerfully. It is very important to search for the "I" that experiences this fear by means of the four essential points. Remember—at this stage the body has been sacrificed, and consciousness has been dissolved into space. Therefore, the "I" that feels threatened appears, yet is not "one with" nor "separate from" the aggregates. In order to recognize this nontrue existence of self, we must correctly recognize the object of negation. This is difficult and requires a great accumulation of merit. If, on analysis, we feel that the "I" is "lost," we are realizing emptiness.

At this point, whichever method of meditation on emptiness we are using, we dissolve all appearances into light and into our hearts. Strongly feeling that all phenomena are empty of inherent existence, we meditate on emptiness single-pointedly. Each of the three ways of meditating on emptiness in Chöd practice is a way to overcome hindrances to the correct view of emptiness.

MARA HINDRANCES IN CHÖD PRACTICE

To overcome hindrances to generating bodhichitta, we should meditate that this moment is the only opportunity to return the kindness of all mother sentient beings, and unshakably keep this motivation throughout practice.

If we lack the proper antidotes of emptiness and bodhichitta, we will not be able to control our minds when frightening appearances manifest. It is considered a sign of progress in this practice if we go unconscious, and then, when we wake up, have forgotten our names and whose bodies we have! This is the ceasing of clinging to the body.

Continually pray to the Three Jewels to realize emptiness. Also, pray to gain realizations of all three vehicles, not just Vajrayana, and to be free from all hindrances to Dharma practice.

In general, there are four types of maras that interfere with Dharma practice: (1) mara of the delusions; (2) mara of the aggregates; (3) devaputra mara; and (4) mara, lord of death.[85]

Mara of the Delusions

Generally speaking, the delusions are not overcome until we realize the state of an arhat.

Mara of the Aggregates

The aggregates are powered by karma and delusion, and are therefore propelled, uncontrollably, into samsara.

Devaputra Mara

According to an Indian commentary to *Ornament of Clear Realization*, "Devaputra" refers to Ishvara, the lord of the desire realm, who controls others' emanations and who hinders practitioners with his arrows. In order to be free of this mara, do we actually destroy Devaputra? Is Devaputra, or Ishvara, animate? If Ishvara were animate, it would follow that there are numberless Ishvaras, as many as there are sentient beings. Is Ishvara inanimate? There is debate concerning this mara's mode of existence.

When we reach the eighth Mahayana spiritual ground, we overcome all maras. Some systems assert Devaputra maras are living beings, and some assert that they are not. There are scriptural references to Ishvara as a being. In the ritual called Four Hundred Practices,[86] forms of maras are made in the aspect of beings, invited, and then requested to depart. If some maras are not beings, why are they requested to leave? In the Prajnaparamita mara-averting ritual, maras are also depicted in animate form.

To perform the Four Hundred Practices we definitely must receive the empowerment called "Buddha, Subduer of Mara."[87] It is valuable as a practice for helping sick people. In order to become qualified to help in this way, we must do a retreat in which the mantra of dependent origination, the YE DHARMA mantra, is recited. Nowadays, some people do this practice without the right empowerment.

Mara, Lord of Death

Dying uncontrollably is the gross form of the mara lord of death. The subtle mara lord of death refers to the practice of bodhisattvas who pass away consciously, taking rebirth in samsara again with intentional control.

In the Chöd system these four maras are identified. Detailed explanations about them can be found in the Prajnaparamita teachings.

There are another four types of maras that Chöd practitioners need to understand and avoid. These four maras are termed obstructive, nonobstructive, joyfulness and arrogance.[88] It is very important to remember these and identify them in Chöd practice, as well as in the sadhana practices of Heruka and Vajrayogini.

Obstructive Maras

The first of these are called "obstructive" maras, meaning maras with material form. When practicing Chöd, interferences may befall us in the form of earth, water, fire, wind, rocks, wild animals, or collapsing houses. If we reach the path of seeing, we are freed from all such dangers. Prior to attainment of the path of seeing we should emulate the Bodhisattva

Sadaprarudita, who endured many painful obstacles and even sacrificed his flesh and blood searching for the guru who would teach him Prajna-paramita. Also remember the trials of purification that Naropa had to endure from his guru, Tilopa. Until we gain the spiritual grounds,[89] we are vulnerable to obstructive maras, so we should not expose ourselves to dangerous places until that time.

Nonobstructive Maras

The next maras are those called "nonobstructive," meaning maras without gross physical form. There are two types: external and internal. Sometimes it is not possible to be certain which of these two types of nonobstructive maras is involved. External, nonobstructive maras usually refer to the harm and disease caused by spirits. It is important to determine whether a disease is caused by the body's elements being out of balance, or by spirits. If it is caused by the elements being out of harmony, we should not be arrogant, thinking we are great practitioners, but should consult a doctor immediately. If, on the other hand, it is a spirit-caused sickness, it can be cured through *tonglen* practice, conjoined with love and compassion.

If someone has a spirit-influenced sickness, we can take that person to a dark room and offer that person's body along with our own as a sacrificial offering by engaging in Chöd. This must be done with the purest motivation of bodhichitta. It is very important in this case to transfer our own and the patient's consciousness both to the deity at the crown of the head. This practice is also done for a corpse prior to its being given to the vultures for "sky-burial," and the merit is dedicated to that body's former consciousness.

Internal nonobstructive maras refer to the three poisons interrupting our Dharma practice. If we do not minimize these delusions, we will be controlled by them. If that happens, Dharma conceit and arrogance arises, and the mind becomes as tough as a scorpion when listening to teachings.

Mara of Joyfulness

The third mara is joyful expectation. This mara is an attitude that exults in thinking that Chöd practice will lead to fame, the power to destroy spirits or cure people, and so on. It reflects mundane concerns for self-aggrandizement, and is attachment to the fruits of practice. This is inappropriate.

Mara of Arrogance

The fourth mara is that of arrogance. This occurs when the thought that we are protected by the empowering blessings of the gurus, yidams, and so forth leads to pride and loss of pure motivation. Instead of Chöd practice severing self-grasping, this mara increases self-grasping.

Whenever we practice Chöd we should feel humble, unprotected, and exposed to spirits. Feeling that spirits could seize us at any moment, we should equalize our feelings, whatever interferences occur. We should be neither pleased nor displeased by these interferences. It is not absolutely necessary to visit a hundred springs or to practice on a high cliff. We *do* need highly qualified places, however, when we have the capacity to meditate in such sites. Wherever we practice, we need the motivation to sacrifice ourselves, free of pride and arrogance. If we are easily frightened, our practice will be constantly interrupted, but if we are too brave, this will hinder our practice also. There was once a Chöd practitioner who was too brave to feel fear. Finally, after trying many places, he decided to spend the night in the "chamber of fear," the protector room at Samye Monastery. This proved too much for him and he fled the next day. We should avoid extremes of timidity and exaggerated bravery. We can do this if we keep the correct motivation at all times and continue to meditate on emptiness, whatever appears to our minds. If violent appearances occur, dissolve them into light and dissolve this light into your heart, meditating on the spacelike emptiness of inherent existence of all phenomena. With proper attitude and mindfulness, we will receive the beneficial results.

The "disturbances"[90] that occur in Chöd practice can be listed as external, internal, and secret. External disturbances are visions of fearful things attacking us, or hearing threats or curses. Internal disturbances are the development of physical ailments or disorders, releasing semen during sleep, or having nightmares. Secret disturbances are the development of desirous attachment, anger, or bewilderment. We need to identify the causes of these disturbances in order to apply the antidotes. If they arise from natural causes, meditate on *lamrim,* and request the guru to minimize the interference. If they arise from spirits, practice *tonglen,* remembering bodhichitta and emptiness at the same time.

There are signs of definite success in overcoming interferences. These are termed the "three severances," external, internal, and secret. We have achieved external severance if we are no longer harmed by nonhuman beings, and, instead, they pay respect to us. We have achieved internal severance if we recover from disease and if, in our dreams, insects and fluids are emitted from our body, or we are offered yogurt or milk. We have achieved secret severance when we destroy the three poisons. We no longer have ambition or hope for results, we no longer have doubts about the practice, and our faith, bodhichitta, and understanding of emptiness have increased.

Appearances to mind can be very disturbing and frightening. There is a pass in Tibet that is marked by a large stone. Not many daytime travelers would notice this stone, but one night there was a man who did. He believed the stone to be a spirit because of its size and shape. Drawing his long sword, he hit the stone and was very surprised when it struck back so hard it blunted his sword!

In Tibet near Damundrag Monastery there was a terrifying charnel ground. Monks would go there to practice Chöd. I have, also. One monk went there to practice, but did not receive any visions at all. As he was returning home, however, stones fell on him. Phara Rinpoche went there to practice, also. He was quite courageous in Chöd practice. Once, when he was practicing there, he saw a black figure with long fingernails perhaps a cubit long. In spite of being very fearful, he continued his practice, but soon lost his place in the sadhana and ran out of energy to play the damaru. Looking at the black figure again, he covered his head with his robe, thinking that he would just let whatever happened, happen. Nothing did, so he gathered his possessions and quietly crept away from the place.

A Sera monk once had a thighbone trumpet wrapped in gold. He used to practice Chöd behind Drepung Monastery. Monks would often play jokes on chöpas. One of his friends decided to test his practice. Hiding behind him, he made a frightening sound. The monk immediately ran off in such a panic that he lost his thighbone and broke his damaru. Feeling guilty, his friend did not admit his prank. The monk was so terrified that, later on, he could not remember which path he had taken, so the thighbone of gold remained lost.

People who deny the existence of spirits may not receive harm from them, but they also may not receive the benefits of Chöd practice. So, sometimes it is good to be a little superstitious!

I wonder why so many Westerners go crazy? What sort of meditation are they doing? With so many distinguished Dharma teachers in the West, why are so many Westerners allowed to remain mentally disturbed, with no one asking qualified lamas[91] for assistance? There are, according to Dharma, five different reasons for insanity: due to karma, disease, frustration and anxiety, intense fear, and possession. If we become mentally disturbed we should rely on our gurus for help and request blessings from them. Lamas can sometimes do rituals to cure insanity if they are asked to do so. Some insanity due to imbalance of the elements can be cured by medical prescriptions from a doctor. Some insanity goes away. In one case, while I was in Buxa, eight or nine monks went crazy due to thinking that Buddhadharma was lost, their country was lost, their family and friends were lost. But they recovered after a few weeks. Our true protection against insanity is not a protection string or an amulet box but meditation on emptiness. Even a rough understanding of emptiness of inherent existence through a generic image can prevent spirits from harming us as long as we hold that understanding. In addition, meditation on emptiness indirectly overcomes many everyday interferences and problems.

DEDICATING THE ACCUMULATIONS TO UNSURPASSED GREAT ENLIGHTENMENT

Dharma practitioners need to know how to dedicate properly. This is like directing a horse with a bridle.

There are five obstacles to pure dedication practice. These five are (1) arrogance; (2) interest in good reputation; (3) anger; (4) wrong view—for instance, dedicating without any faith in the result; and (5) wrong dedication.

A correct dedication is such as the following:

May I become Buddha to benefit all sentient beings!

Other dedications may be for attainment of realizations, sustenance of the Sangha and long lives of the gurus. Whatever the dedication, we should dedicate with awareness of the non-inherent existence of the three spheres of the dedication.[92] If we do this, our roots of virtue will not be eradicated by anger. The pure drop of such a dedication will enter the vast ocean of virtue and the dedication will remain until the effect, buddhahood, is realized. Roots of virtue sustained by wisdom cannot be destroyed by anger. If our dedication is sustained by bodhichitta, for example, but lacks awareness of emptiness of the three spheres, it can be exhausted or destroyed by anger, just as a banana tree is exhausted after bearing limited fruit. This is asserted by Chandrakirti in *Guide to the Middle Way* and by Shantideva in *Guide to the Bodhisattvas' Way of Life*. Both assert that virtues arisen from practices such as giving or moral discipline can be destroyed by anger. In the *Condensed Perfection of Wisdom Sutra,* Buddha says that if a bodhisattva who has not received prophecy of his or her enlightenment becomes angry with a bodhisattva who *has* received such prophecy, a hundred thousand eons of the angry bodhisattva's roots of virtue would be destroyed. If the situation were reversed, only a hundred eons of the angry bodhisattva's roots of virtue would be destroyed. In this way, we should remember the tremendous destructive power of anger and why it is essential that we make pure dedication with wisdom.

The power of dedication is tremendous. When we practice Chöd we should fully offer our bodies out of compassion and make a dedication that, through the power of this practice, we become able to release all beings, both those with and without breath.[93] The dedication in the sadhana was composed by Kachen Yeshe Gyaltsen and compiled by Kyabje Phabongka. If we decide to practice Chöd, we should recite the text as often as we can and make our practice continuous. Learning it conscientiously, we should chant appropriately and play the damaru and thighbone correctly. Alternately, we can practice just the red and white distributions together or separately. Kachen Yeshe Gyaltsen has written commentaries to both these distribution practices. Anyone who has received Machig Labdrön's *Opening the Door of Space* empowerment can use any Chöd text. Gelug practitioners, however, do not generally use the *Precious Garland* sadhana.[94]

USE OF THE RITUAL DAMARU
AND THIGHBONE TRUMPET

PRACTITIONERS MUST KNOW the specifications of the damaru and thighbone trumpet and the way to play them. The damaru should ideally be of Nepalese palsing wood and it should be of a size such that the practitioner's arm can just encircle it with the fingertip touching the chest at the heart. It should be blue, and can be painted if necessary. It should have a belt handle made of red woolen cloth. The belt can be decorated with coral. A Gelug handle should have a five-colored knotted "tail" attached to the end of the handle. The five colors—white, blue, yellow, green, and red— represent the five transcendent wisdoms. The cloth should be plaited so that the colors can be seen. We can also put bells on the cloth to symbolize emptiness. The damaru should also have strings with soft pellet beaters, and a patch to protect the fingers against the handle.

Some practitioners used to tie the hair of corpses, tiger, fox, or squirrel skins to the green and yellow parts of the handle. Certain powers can be gained by doing this, but Gelug practitioners should not do it. What is crucial for pure practitioners is development of love and compassion. Practice, not show! Experience, not appearances!When we play the damaru, it should be played softly and at the height of the face. It should be played towards the body. This was suggested by a Drepung geshe, and Kyabje Phabongka approved it.[95] When playing the damaru prior to visualizing the objects of refuge we recite MA-DANG-LHA-YI-KA-DRO and so forth.[96] In this Ensa system of Chöd, a bell is not played. The sound of the damaru, being a product, should remind us of impermanence and therefore emptiness, whereas the two sides of the drum and the two pellets should remind us of the inseparability of conventional and ultimate truth. We keep the Chöd drum in a case and only use it at night. In Tibetan monasteries damarus are kept very secret and are never exhibited.

The human thighbone trumpet is to measure about twelve finger widths long, excluding the bone's base (which is the knee). The right side of the base should be higher than the other. The right side represents devas, while the left side represents spirits. The edge of the top of the shin should be very sharp; this is the place where the dakinis dance. The right thighbone of a male or the left thighbone of a female is used. When practicing in cemeteries, the male thighbone is used because it gives a better sound. Thighbones of murder victims are not allowed. Sometimes a two-pointed whip was attached to the thighbone to symbolize method and wisdom, but Gelug practitioners of the Ensa system do not decorate the thighbone at all. Some practitioners recite the Prajnaparamita mantra over possessed beings and whip them with these thighbone whips. But Chöd practitioners should not beat spirits. In Kham, another means of exorcism is to play damarus in front of and behind the possessed person. Maybe they would recover from their disease faster if firecrackers were used instead! Before actually blowing the thighbone to attract the spirits, we should tap the mouth of the trumpet with the palm of our right hand three times.

It is very helpful for aspiring practitioners of Chöd to learn how to play the damaru and chant the ritual correctly. There are nine different tunes in this Chöd practice. In Tibet it was customary for practitioners of this Chöd system to wear conch shell earrings and their hair in plaited knots, but this is not necessary for us. The practice of Chöd flourished in Tibet, but in exile there are not many practitioners due to the changed conditions. In south India there is a Chöd center with thirty-five practitioners, and there is a Chöd center being established in Switzerland. It seems that many Americans wish to practice Chöd. In order to practice they must receive the empowerment, the teachings on practice, and the oral transmission of the text.

THE QUALITIES OF BUDDHA AND JE TSONGKHAPA

If we contemplate the good qualities of the Buddhas we will purify our minds and approach the attainment of those good qualities. There are certain Jataka stories, sutra accounts of Buddha's previous lives, that are particularly beneficial for Chöd practitioners to know and to meditate upon.

The bodhisattva who offered his body to the hungry tigress and her four cubs is an important Jataka tale to contemplate. The tigress and her cubs later became Buddha's first five disciples at the first turning of the wheel of Dharma.

Another story to remember is that of the giant turtle. The giant turtle saved the lives of five hundred merchants from a sinking ship and then, while exhausted on the beach, offered its own body to eighty thousand ants. The turtle later became the Buddha, and the eighty thousand ants were eighty thousand devas who attended one of his discourses. As we recall these stories we make strong dedication prayers that all beings who benefit from our practice of Chöd may become our first disciples when buddhahood is attained.

Another Jataka story to remember is that of the bodhisattva "Patient One." Once he was meditating under a bodhi tree. A king and his four queens were traveling in the forest. The king fell asleep after a meal and the four queens went for a walk. They met the bodhisattva and requested teachings from him. When he awoke, the king was alarmed to find that his queens were gone. When the king and his attendants came upon the bodhisattva and the four queens, the queens were so frightened by the king's anger that they ran away. The king was furious and demanded to know what the meditator was doing. When the bodhisattva replied that he was practicing patience the king was so incensed that he cut off the bodhisattva's arm. He asked the meditator if he understood. Receiving the same answer he cut off his other arm. This happened three times more, the king cutting off the bodhisattva's legs and, finally, his head. Throughout this ordeal the bodhisattva prayed that, by the power of his suffering, self-grasping might be totally severed. Later the bodhisattva became Buddha, and the king and his queens became the first five disciples. At one point Buddha asked the disciple who had been the king if he understood, four times. After the fourth time that disciple immediately attained the state of an arhat.

The question may be asked, "If so many buddhas have manifested, why do so many sentient beings remain in samsara?" The answer to this is that if we are not liberated it is our own fault. We are like dry seeds amidst the rainfall. Buddhas have complete power to free us like the sun shining in all directions. But if we are like a cave facing north, we will not receive direct light. Correct faith is required to receive the blessings of the buddhas.

If we wish to be under the blessings and protection of Je Tsongkhapa we must make progress in understanding and actualizing the three principal paths. These are the most important practices of this and all other lifetimes. The practice of Chöd is an ornament to the three principal paths. Practicing both is mutually complementary and extremely beneficial.

To be close to Je Tsongkhapa, we can go to visit him, now. Je Tsongkhapa appeared to Khedrub Je in five different forms. In the last of these he appeared as a mahasiddha on a tiger and said to Khedrub Je, "Prepare to visit me! My mandala is on the Five-Peaked Mountain in China." Je Tsongkhapa resides on this mandala mountain, called Wu Tai Shan, and also in Tushita, Shambhala, and other places. In order to visit these places we must train in the three principal paths, request our lamas for blessings, and view the lama as inseparable from the deity. Few actually visit these places, although it is easy. Some Indian practitioners and Tibetan geshes do visit Tushita and Wu Tai Shan. Wu Tai Shan, in China, has many places of pilgrimage. It is not always clear to pilgrims that there are five peaks there. One lama, before entering the clear light of death, visited Wu Tai Shan and saw meditators, monks, and empty square meditation mats. Apparently, many Tibetans visit there and return to Tibet, leaving their meditation seats there.

In order to visit Tushita and this mountain mandala, we must master the perfections and have great faith in Maitreya, Manjushri, and Je Tsongkhapa. We must begin, however, by reducing our attachment to this life's appearances right now. Pray to attain the first of the three principal paths, renunciation, as soon as possible!

Colophon

These Chöd teachings by Kyabje Zong Rinpoche were given in April 1984 at Manjushri Institute, Conishead Priory, Ulverston, Cumbria, U.K. and were translated by Tenzin Paksam. They were first transcribed and edited by Keith and Julia Milton. Then, under the direction of Kyabje Zong Chogtrul Rinpoche, assisted by Venerable Geshe Losang Tsultrim, they were reedited by David Molk.

May all readers find the essence of this book!
—Venerable Zong Rinpoche Tenzin Wangdag

Zong Labrang
Gaden Monastic University
P.O. Tibetan Colony - 581411
Mundgod, Distt North Kanara
Karnataka State, INDIA

email: zongrtw@yahoo.com

Appendices

Translations by David Molk

Dedicating the Illusory Body as Ganachakra:
Promoting the Experience of Means and Wisdom, Wealth of the Ganden Practice Lineage[97]

KYABJE PHABONGKA DECHEN NYINGPO

NAMO GURU BHYA

With deep reverence I pay homage and go for refuge at the lotus feet of the Precious Venerable Guru whose kindness is unequaled! With great affection, please care for me!

Here, a fortunate person who keeps as their innermost meditation the precious conventional and ultimate bodhichittas, in order to bring about an exceptional boost to their practice of the profound, engages in practice of the instructions coming from the Ganden Ear-to-Ear Whispered Lineage of Chöd, the profound instructions on Severance of Mara. From such sources as the Manjushri teachings, the root commentary to the Chöd Instruction Guide for Those Seeking Liberation,[98] *and* Ornament to the Ganden Practice Lineage Teachings,[99] *you must inform yourself as to place of practice and basis of Practice: that is, the qualifications required of a person who does the practice, the instructions as to how to practice, and on the basis of having practiced, how signs of disturbance and resolution occur. Herein are arranged just the verses appropriate for regular recitation. To set one's motivation for going to a charnel ground or haunted place and to go by way of the "four modes" and so on, recite:*

(The three overwhelmings are performed here. Relating to the overwhelming of gods and ghosts, the following recitation is added from the oral tradition:

Fragile spirits! Don't be afraid!
Don't be averse or at all afraid!

Blow the thighbone trumpet in a long tone once, thinking, "Worldly dakinis, gods and ghosts, listen!" Blowing it again, once long and once short, think, "Worldly dakinis, gods and ghosts, come here!" Blowing it the third time, once long and twice short, think, "Worldly dakinis, gods and ghosts, come here, gather here!"

Relating to the overwhelming of self, the oral tradition adds:

All virtuous phenomena are overwhelmed in the birthless,
ceaseless sphere!
All harmful phenomena are overwhelmed in the birthless,
ceaseless sphere!
May the billion worlds, all realms of the universe, be pervaded
by my great illumination!)

PHAT
Well remembering Buddha's previous lives,
To take the great essence from this body,
Expelling the eight mundane concerns,
Like disdaining and enslaving gods and ghosts.

PHAT
All mother beings, 'specially gods and ghosts
I'll free from samsara and two obstructions.
Since appearances are primordially void,
Illusion's dance counters mind's creations.

The brave tiger's walk

PHAT
I generate divine pride of Heruka.
Above, the Gurus and Three Jewels gather like clouds.

Hosts of heroes line up on the right.
Behind are hosts of Dharma Protectors.
I go, controlling the path's right side with skillful means.
I go, keeping great bliss as the heart of the path.
I go, drawing the path's gods and ghosts to me.
I go, setting all, as well, on the path to enlightenment.

The yogini's profound walk

PHAT
I generate divine pride of Vajrayogini.
Above, the Gurus and Three Jewels gather like clouds.
Hosts of dakinis flock to the left.
Behind are hosts of Dharma Protectors.
I go, controlling the path's left side with wisdom.
I go, seeing with the wisdom eye of emptiness.
I go, drawing the path's gods and ghosts to me.
I go, setting all, as well, on the path to enlightenment.

Walk of the coiling black snake

PHAT
I generate divine pride of Vajrayogini.
Above, the Gurus and Three Jewels gather like clouds.
Hosts of heroes line up on the right.
Hosts of heroines flock to the left.
Behind are hosts of Dharma Protectors.
I go, controlling the path's right and left sides.
I go, herding the path's gods and ghosts like cattle.
I go, setting all, as well, on the path to enlightenment.

Walk of the dakinis' dance

PHAT
I generate divine pride of Heruka.

Above, the Gurus and Three Jewels gather like clouds.
Hosts of heroes line up on the right.
Hosts of heroines flock to the left.
Behind are hosts of Dharma Protectors.
I go, controlling the path's center by dancing.
I go, thinking of the gods and ghosts' fear and affliction.
I go, setting all, as well, on the path to enlightenment.

Going by way of the four modes

PHAT
Body as corpse, mind as corpse bearer,
Place, charnel ground, gods and ghosts, jackals,
Mind parting from matter, with emptiness mixed,
I go, giving up hope and fear's demon hosts!

Going in that manner, at the site perform visualizations of the three "overwhelmings" as instructed in the commentary, thus completing the preliminary stages.

The actual practice includes the session and the session break. The first includes the preliminary stage of training one's continuum by way of the four "great guides"; the actual practice of gathering the two accumulations to place imprints for the two kayas; and dedicating the roots of virtue gathered to unexcelled great enlightenment. The preliminary stage has four parts: the guide to refuge and bodhichitta that make one's continuum a worthy vessel; the guide to Guru Yoga that inspires one with blessings; the guide to seven-limb prayer with mandala offering that brings gathering of the accumulations; and the guide to descent of nectar from AH that purifies harm and obscuration.

Refuge and bodhichitta

PHAT
In the fore space, on lion throne, lotus and moon,
Guru, Great Mother Labkyi Drönma stands.
Root and lineage Gurus, Yidams, Three Jewels and
Dharma Guardian multitudes encircle her.

I and all beings through space take refuge
In root and lineage Gurus, Yidams and
Supreme Refuges, Buddha, Dharma and
Sangha 'till gaining highest enlightenment. (3x)

To free beings drowning in suffering's ocean,
Wishing to attain supreme enlightenment,
Wholeheartedly I'll train without despair
In all time's Sugatas' Children's[100] deeds. (3x)

Guru Yoga that inspires with blessings

PHAT
On my crown on lotus and sun mandala is
Labkyi Drönma, supreme Guru, inseparable,
Aspect, Vajravarahi, red in hue,
Right hand holds curved knife and left a blood-filled skullcup.

Armpit well adorned with a khatvanga,
Fiercely smiling, fangs bared, wearing bone ornaments,
Naked, hair loose, amidst blazing rays of light,
Standing, right leg bent, left outstretched, at her three places,

Marked by three letters, light rays from the letter HUM
Invoke unimpeded from their natural place,
Vajrayogini surrounded by infinite hosts
Of peaceful and wrathful ones who become nondual.

Again from the heart's HUM light radiates,
Gathering, with force, harmers, spirits, interferers,
And all six realms' sentient beings to settle around me,
Like swans gathering around a lotus pond.

Blow the thighbone trumpet three times

*Seven-limb prayer with mandala offering that brings
gathering of the accumulations*

PHAT
From truth body spontaneous great bliss play,
Rising exquisite with enchanting grace,
Glorious One, charming those fixed in three realms,
Homage Guru Vajravarahi!

Three gifts, outer, inner, secret, and suchness,
Three doors' harms and obscurations I confess.
I rejoice in all three times' pure virtues.
Pray teach three vehicles for migrators.
Please remain permanent in three natures.
Through all virtue may the three bodies be gained.

Mandala offering

On my skin, the great and powerful golden ground,
Is sprinkled my blood and oils as scented nectar.
'Midst entrails, iron mountains, limbs, four continents,
My spine becomes Mount Meru, heaped with jeweled atoms.

Two eyes, sun and moon; the two ears are
Parasol and victory banner; heart, wish-fulfilling jewel—
Outer flesh and inner organs all transform
Into perfect enjoyments of humans and gods.

This pure mandala, a wish-fulfilling sea,
To Gurus, Yidams, and Buddhas, Bodhisattvas,
And mighty Guardian oceans well offered, thus,
Kindly accepting, grant blessings and attainments!

IDAM GURU RATNA MANDALAKAM NIRYATAYAMI

Descent of nectar from AH purifying harm and obscuration

PHAT
Founder Buddha, Revered Manjushri and
Aryadeva, sole father Padampa and
Father tantra, method lineage Gurus,
I beseech you, may you bless my mind!

Perfect Wisdom Mother, Revered Tara,
Sukhasiddhi, Machig Labdrön and
Mother tantra, wisdom lineage Gurus,
I beseech you, may you bless my mind!

Founder Buddha, Revered Maitreya,
Arya Asanga, brother Vasubandhu and
The son tantra, union lineage Gurus,
I beseech you, may you bless my mind!

Great Vajradhara, Revered Manjushri,
Pawo Dorje, Losang Dragpa and
Close lineage, blessed lineage Gurus,
I beseech you, may you bless my mind!

Jampel Gyatso, Baso Chögyen and
Chökyi Dorje, Gyalwa Ensapa,
Sangye Yeshe, Losang Chögyen, O
I beseech you, may you bless my mind!

Losang Damchö, Losang Yeshe and
Trinle Chöpel, Losang Namgyal and
Yeshe Gyaltsen, Losang Chöjor, O
I beseech you, may you bless my mind!

Yeshe Tenzin, Thubten Gyatso and
Yeshe Döndrub, Tenzin Khedrub and

Kelsang Khedrub, Jampel Lhundrub, O
I beseech you, may you bless my mind!

In Dharma's sublime land, Dechen Tashi,
Blissful Manjushri's teachings' supreme pillar,
Compassion and love's lord, Dechen Nyingpo,
I beseech you, may you bless my mind![101]

There, at Mochog Tashi Dechen Gönpa,
Guided by Kyabje Phabongka, Lord of Beings,
Revered Yeshe Jampa Rinpoche, O
I beseech you, may you bless my mind!

Clear deep wisdom nondual from bliss expanse,
Sounding PHAT proclaiming the unborn's deep sense,
Showing the supreme path, Losang Tsöndru,
I beseech you, may you bless my mind!

Granting undefiled bliss, Guru Yogini,
Undeceiving Gurus, Yidams, Three Rare Jewels,
And oceans of mighty Dharma Guardians,
I beseech you, may you bless my mind!

Bless me to mentally give up this life,
To train in renunciation, bodhi-mind,
And to realize ultimate selflessness,
Bless me to succeed in the practice of Chöd!

Thus, having beseeched the Guru Deva,
From the body amassed light and nectar flow,
Enter me and others, purifying all
Disease, spirits, evil and obscuration.
Projection free, mind's true nature's revealed!

AH (21x)

Having made requests with heartfelt longing, recite AH twenty-one times. Visualize that at the heart of the Bhagavati is the wisdom being, Great Mother Prajnaparamita, at whose heart is a moon mandala with an AH standing on it. From the AH nectar flows down entering the bodies and minds of myself and others, cleansing all negativity, obscurations, disease, harmful spirits, and obstructers. Secondly, the actual practice of gathering the two accumulations to place imprints for the two kayas has two parts: gathering the accumulation of merit by offering the illusory body, and gathering the accumulation of wisdom through meditation on emptiness. The first includes the white distribution— offering the refined body parts transformed into nectar; the red distribution—giving the leftover flesh and blood; the manifold distribution—transforming the skin into all desirable objects and distributing them; and the giving of dharma and tonglen meditation.

White distribution

PHAT
From my crown down to my navel, avadhuti,[102]
White out, red in, width of a bamboo arrow,
In it, at my navel, my mind in form of a drop,
In aspect being about to leap and fly up,
Through the path of the supreme avadhuti,
Entering the supreme Guru Deva's heart.

PHAT (5x)

My old body, fallen down, abandoned,
White and shining form covers the billion worlds.

PHAT
My mind from the heart of the Guru Deva
Showing dakini aspect, holding curved knife,
Like a vulture circling over meat, I swoop down,
Slit the body with my knife from crown to crotch.

From heart to tips of right and left hands, I cut,
From crotch to tips of right and left feet I cut.

The peeled skin is spread out, reddish in color,
Above it, three-human-head tripod, over it

Is placed the severed skull and into it are poured
Brains, juice, marrow, and all refined body parts.
With curved knife stirring it 'round three times to the right,
It becomes healing, life, and wisdom nectar.

OM AH HUM (3x)

PHAT
Heart dakinis scoop up with a skull
Stainless nectar oceanic offering clouds.
Offered to hosts of root and lineage gurus,
Bless me to practice a stainless lifetime's deeds.

Offered as torma to Yidams and Dakinis,
Pray grant attainments, common and supreme.
Offered revered guests, Three Rare Supreme Jewels,
Pray free from samsara and nirvana's fears.

Offered in thanks to Protectors, qualified guests,
Bless me to accomplish yogic actions well.
Giving it to the poor guests, six realms' beings,
May kindness be returned, you be free from pain.

Red distribution

PHAT
The leftover flesh, blood, bones amassed,
Fills the billion worlds and becomes unending.
My mind illumined as wisdom dakini
Waving curved knife to the sky, this I proclaim.

Thighbone trumpet (3x)

PHAT

From samsara's peak down to the hells,
Gathered gods and ghosts, whatever appear and exist,
'Specially harmers, demons, obstructers and
Local spirits, have loving minds and come here!

Blow the thighbone trumpet (3x)

PHAT

All you here gathered gods and ghosts, listen!
Without fighting, without overpowering each other,
Enjoy this flesh-blood body, like a mountain,
In manner of mother and child for each other!

PHAT

Those of a type who like meat, eat meat!
Those of a type who like blood, drink blood!
Gods and ghosts who like bones, chew on bones!
Enjoy the organs and so on, as you please!

PHAT

All whatever gathered gods and ghosts here,
Enjoying this deluded flesh-blood body,
Give up evil harmful minds toward all and
Actualize love and compassion!

Manifold distribution

My skin cut in pieces becomes silver, gold,
Rich cloth, grain, medicine, mansions, jewelry, clothing,
Bedding, or whatever each of you desires,
Thus, may you be satisfied and take it with you!

Giving of dharma and tonglen meditation

All these beings have been my parents.
To return their begininglesss kind care,
Having pleased them giving my material form,
Also, giving Dharma, I shall free them.

Thus, all compounded things are impermanent.
Also, all that's deluded is suffering in nature.
All is just selfless dependent arising.
Meditating on this, you'll gain peace of nirvana.

Commit not the slightest harmful nonvirtue!
Persevere in performing perfect virtue!
As for your mind, thoroughly subdue it!
Strive to practice this, the teaching of Buddha!

Beings' harms, suffering, two obscurations and such,
In aspect of poisons, weapons, and black light,
Thunderstorms, hail, scorpions, such ugly forms
I now take into the center of my heart.

My body, wealth, collected virtue and such
Become fine things that fulfill beings' wishes, all Buddhas'
Cessations, realizations, and blessings;
Receiving these without effort, may they now be free.

Requesting departure

PHAT
Having thus ripened and released beings
Through giving of material body and Dharma,
Return to your homes in earth, sky, mountain, valley,
Water, rocks, and become altruistic!

Gathering the accumulation of wisdom through meditation on emptiness

As the great Seventh Dalai Lama has said,

> *Looking inwards, body and mind in no way exist as the "harmed"!*
> *Looking outwards, harmers are like striped ropes taken for snakes!*
> *May I be certain that holding mere relative labels*
> *To truly exist are my mind's hallucinations!*

With strong ascertainment of the view thus explained:

PHAT
Giving's three spheres are just labeled names and sounds
And exist, not even an atom, from their sides,
Though all living and inanimate things appear to
Exist truly, they're empty, like illusions.

PHAT
Though things' natures are free of projections,
Various emanated conventions appear.
EVAM's union of wisdom-means, may it bring
Truth and form bodies, free of obscuration!

In isolation, praised by the Buddhas, holding as
Foundation Shakyamuni's pure moral code,
With sharp weapon of wisdom and means' union,
May self-cherishing's root swiftly be cut!

'Midst dense clouds of strong compassion proclaiming
Unborn dependent rising with thund'rous PHAT
Through meteoric blazing great fire of voidness,
May dualism's rock mountain soon be destroyed!

On wings of the two accumulations, unified,
Soaring in space of Bodhisattvas' great deeds,
Staying not in samsara and nirvana's wasteland,
May I swiftly enter Three Kayas' ocean!

Thus, seal the practice with strong prayers and dedications. Practice for between sessions and "subsequent severance" should be learned from such texts as the Chöd Instructions Guide for Those Seeking Liberation *and* Ornament to the Ganden Practice Lineage Teachings. *This,* "Promoting the Experience of Means and Wisdom," *is an arrangement of just the recited portion of* Guide for Those Seeking Liberation *to make it convenient for chanting in verse. Something of this nature was requested by the nun Jampa Dekyong of Tsetang Zarshi. It was composed by the ordained Phabongka Tulku Jampa Tenzin Trinle Gyatso without polluting the oral instructions of the Ear-to-Ear Whispered Ensa Lineage, so that it would be easy for beginners. May all be auspicious!*

Chöd mind training prayer[103]

My Founder, the Buddha Bhagavan, on the
Occasion of the path of great courage,
When he was the Prince Total Freedom, he gave
His own son, his daughter, and his royal domain;
Likewise, may I be able to give my so cherished
Retinue and enjoyments without regret.

When he was King Great Courage
He fed the tigress his own flesh; likewise, may I
Be able to give this cherished illusory
Body gladly to the hosts of flesh eaters!

When he was the Prince Power of Love
He fed his own blood to the yakshas; so may I
Be able to give my own warm heart's blood,
So hard to part from, with love, to the blood drinkers!

When he was the Merchant's Son irrigating water,
He freed fish by saying Tathagatas' names;
So may I be able to give holy Dharma
To all beings who're destitute of the Teachings!

When he was the Prince Great Virtue
He bore betrayal with great compassion; likewise,
When my circle perversely disturbs me, may I
Specially cherish them with great compassion!

When he was the Monkey Bodhisattva
He rescued the evil man from the well;
So may I not despair helping evil beings,
Not seeking help, guiding them with compassion!

Alas! No being has not been my parents,
There's nowhere a happy moment in samsara;
Thus, all gods and ghosts among my parents,
May I be able to guide you from samsara!

Whatever spirits are still left here,
Whether dwelling in the earth or in the sky,
May I always have great love for beings and
May they all enjoy the Dharma, day and night!

Buddha, supreme of the great, unexcelled,
Through Buddha, the Sun Lord of Dharma's blessings
Calming the foe, maras, and hinderers; may night and
Day be always glorious and auspicious!

Dharma, supreme, sublime truth, unexcelled,
Through holy Dharma amrita's blessing,
Calming the foe, tormenting delusions; may night and
Day be always glorious and auspicious!

Sangha's precious qualities blazing, through Bodhisattvas'
Beneficial deeds' truth's blessings,
Increasing virtuous collections, faultless; may night and
Day be always glorious and auspicious!

Offering Ganachakra in Connection with the Yoga
of the Profound Path of Chöd

WRITTEN AND COMPILED BY
KYABJE ZONG RINPOCHE LOSANG TSÖNDRU

OM SVASTI

Here, made easy for beginners to follow, is arranged the way to offer Ganachakra in connection with the yoga of the profound path of Chöd.[104] *Be informed as to the place of practice, the basis of practice, the signs of uprising and resolution resulting from practice, and so forth, from the scriptures and the oral instructions of your Guru. Arrange all of the requisites for Ganachakra, and set your motivation. Then, visualizing the Refuges, begin to recite:*

In space ahead, on a vast throne raised by eight great lions, on a multicolored thousand-petalled lotus and moon cushion, is Machig Labkyi Drönma, inseparable from my Guru. At her heart is Great Mother Prajnaparamita. Above is Buddha Vajradhara; to the right, the Yamantaka mandala deities; to the left, the Chakrasamvara deities; in front, the Guhyasamaja deities; and, in back, the deities of Hevajra. Encircling them are the divine hosts of root and lineage Gurus, Yidams, Buddhas, Bodhisattvas, Heroes, Heroines, and Dharma Protectors. Before each of them are their eloquently expressed Teachings in the aspect of scriptures. Their various emanations pervade all of the space beyond them. Below are all sentient beings, including those with harmful intentions.

Feeling my own intense dread of lower realms' and samsaric sufferings; empathetic compassion unable to bear the samsaric torment of all mother and father sentient beings, including those such as ghosts and demons; and deep heartfelt conviction in the Three Jewels' unique power to alleviate those sufferings...

PHAT
Well remembering Buddha's previous lives,
To take the great essence from this body,
Expelling the eight mundane concerns,
Like disdaining and enslaving gods and ghosts.

PHAT
All mother beings, 'specially gods and ghosts,
I'll free from samsara and two obstructions.
Since appearances are primally void,
Illusion's dance counters mind's creations.

(The following recitations are added from the oral tradition:

The overwhelming of gods and ghosts

> Fragile spirits! Don't be afraid!
> Don't be averse or at all afraid!

The overwhelming of self

> All virtuous phenomena are overwhelmed in the birthless,
>   ceaseless sphere!
> All harmful phenomena are overwhelmed in the birthless,
>   ceaseless sphere!
> May the billion worlds, all realms of the universe, be pervaded
>   by my great illumination!

To benefit beings, I wish to attain the peace of incomparable
   enlightenment. Therefore, this body that others find hard
   to part with
I freely give with compassion of unvacillating wisdom.
May I be cared for by the Bodhisattvas and soon attain perfect
   enlightenment!
I shall liberate the three realms from the terrors of the ocean
   of samsara!

Beyond speech, thought, expression, wisdom gone beyond
Unborn, unceasing, with a nature like space,
Discerning transcendent wisdom's sphere of awareness,
Homage to the Mother of the three times' Buddhas!

TAYATA OM GATE GATE PARAGATE PARASAMGATE
BODHI SVAHA)

Here, begin playing the damaru and bell in nine beats, twice, reciting the GATE mantra of the Heart Sutra. *Next, play the MA-DANG-LHA-YI-KA-DRO rhythm twice, the CHOM-DEN-DE rhythm twice, then, MA-DANG-KA-DRO twice, and the MA-DANG twice. Then, following the chant leader, ring the bell in time with the words. The chant leader begins and the assembly follows, playing the DRUM-DRUM rhythm:*

PHAT
Supreme Captains guiding all the fortunate to freedom,
In root and lineage Gurus, I take refuge.

Door to every highest siddhi without exception,
In the hosts of Yidams, I take refuge.

Unexcelled Founder, fully realized and perfected,
In Buddha, the Awakened, I take refuge.

Glorious supreme "separation from attachment,"
In valid holy Dharma, I take refuge.

Perfect companions and leaders, always virtuous,
In Sangha, the supreme host, I take refuge.

Until attaining the essence of enlightenment,
In you, holy best of fields, I take refuge.

As I do well honor you with profound devotion,
Compassionate Protectors, please accept me!

To free beings drowning in suffering's ocean,
Wishing to attain supreme enlightenment,
Wholeheartedly I'll train without despair
In all times' Sugatas' Children's deeds. (3x)

Guru Yoga

PHAT
On my crown on lotus and sun mandala is
Labkyi Drönma, supreme Guru, inseparable;
Aspect, Vajravarahi, red in hue,
Right hand holds curved knife and left a blood-filled skullcup.

Armpit well adorned with a khatvanga,
Fiercely smiling, fangs bared, wearing bone ornaments,
Naked, hair loose, amidst blazing rays of light,
Standing, right leg bent, left outstretched, at her three places,

Marked by three letters, light rays from the letter HUM
Invoke unimpeded from their natural place,
Vajrayogini surrounded by infinite hosts
Of peaceful and wrathful ones who become nondual.

Seven-limb prayer

PHAT
Sphere of truth, projection free, spontaneous,
Play of perfect enjoyment of great bliss,
And many, various emanated Dakinis,
Homage to Buddha Vajravarahi!

Offered to delight you, pray accept them,
In expanse of space of inborn bliss-voidness,
Clouds of offerings bearing undefiled bliss,
In a thousand expressions of perfection!

Though all are primordially pure by nature,
Conditioned by beginningless unknowing,
All collected, dreamlike faults I purify
In sphere of pure nature, inexpressible!

Though the ultimate, beyond speech, thought, expression,
Is without sign of virtue and nonvirtue,
We rejoice with all our hearts in all relative
Virtues, as pure and clear as moon crystal!

Empty of true existence yet, like echoes sounding,
To exhort beings like myself to the good path,
Never leaving us until end of existence,
Please stay with us for ages beyond counting!

From gathered energy thus appearing yet empty,
Whatever positive potential comes forth,
To free all nontruly existent wanderers,
I dedicate to Vajradhara Union!

The brief seven-limb prayer may be substituted for the longer version here, as follows:

PHAT
From truth body spontaneous great bliss play,
Rising exquisite with enchanting grace,
Glorious One, charming those fixed in three realms,
Homage, Guru Vajravarahi!

Three gifts, outer, inner, secret, and suchness,
Three doors' harms and obscurations I confess.
I rejoice in all three times' pure virtues.
Pray teach three vehicles for migrators.
Please remain permanent in three natures.
Through all virtue may the three bodies be gained.

Mandala offering

*To offer the mandala elaborately, visualize your mind in the aspect of a drop inside
your central channel at the navel. Recite PHAT four times, visualizing your mind drop
rising from navel to heart, heart to throat, throat to crown, and from the crown dissolving into the heart of the Guru above. Again, recite PHAT once more as your mind
emerges from the heart of the Guru in the aspect of a green Karmadakini. Done less
elaborately, the recitation of PHATs may be omitted.*

On my skin, the great and powerful golden ground,
Is sprinkled my blood and oils as scented nectar.
'Midst entrails, iron mountains, limbs, four continents,
My spine becomes Mount Meru, heaped with jeweled atoms.

Two eyes, sun and moon; the two ears are
Parasol and victory banner; heart, wish-fulfilling jewel—
Outer flesh and inner organs all transform
Into perfect enjoyments of humans and gods.

This pure mandala, a wish-fulfilling sea,
To Gurus, Yidams, and Buddhas, Bodhisattvas,
And mighty Guardian oceans well offered, thus,
Kindly accepting, grant blessings and attainments!

IDAM GURU MANDALAKAM NIRYATAYAMI

Descent of nectar from AH purifying harm and obscuration

(One may recite just the requests to the Gurus of the Close Lineage or, extensively, with damaru in the DRUM-DRUM or CHOM-DEN-DE rhythm.)

PHAT
In palace of Dharmakaya's stainless sphere,
Mother Prajnaparamita, I beseech:

Please bless me to sever self-grasping's bondage,
To train in love, compassion, and bodhi-mind,
And, through Mahamudra path of union,
To quickly attain supreme enlightenment.

Extensively, the previous four lines may be repeated after each request. In brief form, they may be recited once at the end of the requests.

There, at your abode of Vulture's Peak Mountain,
Supreme Founder Shakyamuni, I beseech!

There, in the Pure Land of Turquoise Leaves,
Revered Arya Tara, I beseech!

In the Dharma Pure Land of Tushita,
Regent Buddha Maitreya, I beseech!

In infinite realms throughout space,
Wisdom Arya Manjushri, I beseech!

In palace of swirling rainbow light,
Sukhasiddhi Dakini, I beseech!

On Indian mountain Kukkutapada[105]
Master Arya Asanga, I beseech!

At Nalanda in central India,
Second Buddha[106] Vasubandhu, I beseech!

In your hut of grass abode in India,
Master Aryadeva, I beseech!

In your Latö Dingri Langkor abode,
Mahasiddha Dampa Sangye, I beseech!

In hermitage of Lhasa's valley meadows,
Kyotön Sönam Lama, I beseech!

At your remote Zangri Karmar home,
Machig, chief of Dakinis, I beseech![107]

In your monastery of Nyemo Ku,
Revered Kugom Chöseng, I beseech!

In Lungme Changra hermitage,
Revered Dölpa Zangtal, I beseech!

At the supreme site of the River Mountain,
Mahasiddha Gyanag Cherbu, I beseech!

At home above Radrong Seway Ling,
Revered Sangye Rabtön, I beseech!

At home on Zalmo's rocky mountainside,
Elder Sangye Gelong, I beseech!

In the palace of Karag Munkang,
Revered Sumpa Repa, I beseech!

At the glorious Rigong hermitage,
Beings' Protector, Sangye Tönpa, I beseech!

At Nyangtö Samling Monastery,
Revered Khedrub Chöje, I beseech!

At the hermitage of Latö Pukar,
Revered Togden Ögyal, I beseech!

At hermitage of Dragkar Chölung,
Revered Tashi Gyaltsen, I beseech!

At the hermitage of Lhabu Gyal,
Revered Kunga Yeshe, I beseech!

Without fixed abode in secluded retreats,
Revered Samten Dorje, I beseech!

At glorious Gyalchen hermitage,
Peerless Gyaltsen Palzang, I beseech!

At glorious Gökung hermitage,
Revered Sherab Drubpa, I beseech!

At the Tashilhunpo Vihara,
Most learned Lungrig Gyatso, I beseech!

At the Riwo Gepel hermitage,
Refuge Thubten Namgyal, I beseech!

Up to here has been the long lineage, which continues below from Gyalwa Ensapa onwards. To make requests to the close lineage, continue with melody and damaru as before, or else use the RANG-TA melody with the MA-DANG-LHA-YI-KA-DRO rhythm.

PHAT
In Akanishta Dharma Palace,
All pervasive Vajradhara, I beseech!

In mansion of great bliss Dharmakaya,
Bhagavati Vajravarahi, I beseech!

At the Five-peaked Mountain of China,
Manjushri, Treasure of Wisdom, I beseech!

In Manjushri's practice mandala,
Revered Pawo Dorje, I beseech!

At peerless glorious Ganden Mountain
Conqueror Losang Dragpa, I beseech!

In Maldro Pangsay Monastery,
Togden Jampel Gyatso, I beseech!

In Baso, spontaneous great bliss abode,
Baso Chökyi Gyaltsen, I beseech!

In mansion abode of lotus light,
Mahasiddha Chökyi Dorje, I beseech!

From this point, the long and close lineages converge:

There, in your Ensa Dharma Palace,
Gyalwa Losang Döndrub,[108] I beseech!

In blissful palace of three Kayas,
Master Siddha Sangye Yeshe, I beseech!

At the seat of those prior great Siddhas,
Revered Losang Chögyen, I beseech!

In isolated Kechari retreat,
Supreme Siddha Könchog Gyaltsen, I beseech!

There in remote Chuwar Dharma castle,
Lhatsun Losang Dorje, I beseech!

In unfixed isolated retreats,
Revered Trinle Chöpel, I beseech!

In the great cave of virtue of Kyirong,
Highest Siddha Losang Namgyal, I beseech!

At site of Tsechog Ling Monastery,
Tutor Yeshe Gyaltsen, I beseech!

In retreat in remote haunted places,
Lord of adepts, Losang Chöjor, I beseech!

At the Tsechog Lama's monastic seat,
Dülzin Yeshe Tenzin, I beseech!

At Zhide Monastery's fasting temple,
Revered Thubten Gyatso, I beseech!

There, at the college of Dagpo Shedrub Ling,
Spiritual Friend Yeshe Döndrub, I beseech!

In Jor region remote retreat,
Tutor Jampa Kunkyab, I beseech!

At Yangön Hermitage on Lhading Mountain,
Bodhisattva Kelsang Tenzin, I beseech!

In isolation on Lhading Mountain,
Lord of Adepts Tenzin Khedrub, I beseech!

In retreat at remote sites of Phartsang,
Kyabje Jampel Lhundrub, I beseech!

There in the pure realm of Tashi Chöling,
Lord of Refuge, Dechen Nyingpo, I beseech!

At the Mochog Great Bliss Hermitage,
Revered Yeshe Jampa, I beseech!

At Ganden Monastery, in great Dharma dance,
Revered Losang Tsöndru, I beseech!

Forever, on lotus and moon at my crown,
Guru Bhagavati, I beseech!

In mansion of my own mind's pure light,
Guru, Yidam, Three Refuges, I beseech!

There, at the supreme twenty-four sites,
Three place's Heroes and Dakinis, I beseech!

At sites of the eight great charnel grounds,
Mighty Protectors of Dharma, I beseech!

There, retreating in remote haunted sites,
Vajra brothers and sisters, I beseech!

Please bless me to sever self-grasping's bondage,
To train in love, compassion and bodhi-mind,
And, through Mahamudra path of union,
To quickly attain supreme enlightenment.

PHAT
Bless me to correctly rely on the Guru!
Bless me to know how rare is this human birth!
Bless me to use this life for highest purpose!
Bless me to remember death comes any time!
Bless me to realize that I've no time to waste!

Bless me to give up all of this life's concerns!
Bless me to have faithful belief in Dharma!
Bless me to firmly renounce this samsara!
Bless me to stay in retreat in frightful sites!
Bless me to take bad conditions on the path!
Bless me to see inconvenience as helpful!
Bless me so sickness gives a boost to practice!
Bless me to develop love and compassion!
Bless me to be able to cherish others!
Bless me to cast off this body to be food!
Bless me to inspire gods and ghosts to Dharma!
Bless me to train in supreme bodhichitta!
Bless me to realize emptiness, extreme free!
Bless me to meditate without laxity!
Bless me to sever self-grasping from the root!
Bless me to be successful in Chöd practice!
Bless me to achieve my own and others' goals![109]
Bless me to attain the two types of siddhi!
Bless me to be free of pride in all of these!
Bless me to still the four maras on the spot!
Bless me to manifest the Triple Kaya!
Bless me to gain control of all existence!
Bless me to make all connections meaningful!

*Through the power of having made such fervent requests, purifying streams
of nectar flow down:*

Through such intense devotion,
And power of these focused prayers,
From the Guru Deva's heart,
Immense light and nectar flows.
Bathing the body, it clears
Sickness, spirits, harms, and blocks,
Especially, self-grasping
And self-cherishing are cleansed.

Life, merit and learning grow,
Two bodhichittas, most of all!

AH (21x)

*Chant these slowly, visualizing purification through the flow of nectar,
playing the damaru in the DRUM-DRUM rhythm:*

Mid-body is avadhuti,
Width of a bamboo arrow,
At the heart center, my mind
As a drop, ready to fly,
Up through the central channel,
Reaching Guru Deva's heart,
Becoming bliss-void Dharmakaya!

PHAT (4x)

*With the first PHAT, one's consciousness rises from the heart to the throat; with the
next, from the throat to the crown; and, with the third PHAT, from the crown to the
heart of the Guru. With the fourth PHAT, the old body collapses on the ground. With
the next PHAT, below, one's consciousness emerges from the Guru's heart in dakini
aspect.*

PHAT
Again, in Guru Deva's form,
Swooping down like vulture upon meat,
Cutting the body, flesh, blood, and bones,
Are poured in tripod-based kapala,
Blessed with my knife's three stirs to the right,
Becomes life, healing, wisdom nectar.

OM AH HUM (3x)

Saying this and contemplating as described, bless the substances. Then, to bless beings and the environment, recite:

EH MA HO
Great sport of wisdom,
All domains are vajra fields,
Abodes, vajra palaces,
Seas of offering clouds blaze forth.

Objects have all wished glory,
Real viras, virinis, beings,
Not even deception's name,
All is just endlessly pure.

Next, bless the offerings actually arranged for Ganachakra, playing the damaru in DRUM-DRUM rhythm:

HUM Within empty truth body,
O'er stirred wind and blazing fire
On three-human-head tripod,
AH In a fit skull kapala,
OM Each substance brightly appears.
Over these is OM AH HUM.
 All with brilliant colors blaze.
Wind moves, fire burns, contents melt.
By boiling, vapors pour forth,
Sending the three letters' light
To ten sides, thus inviting
The three vajras with nectars.
 All fuse in, the letters three,
Melt to nectar, it's all mixed,
Cleansed, changed, increased, EH MA HO
To a bright sea of delights.

OM AH HUM (3x)

Blowing the thighbone trumpet three times, visualize inviting all the guests for the offerings. Play the damaru in MA-DANG-LHA-YI-KA-DRO rhythm:

PHAT
Nature compassion, root and lineage Gurus,
Hosts of Yidams, Three Jewels of Refuge,
Heroes, Dakinis, Dharma Protectors,
Invited, pray come to this offering site!

'Midst seas of offering clouds, outer and inner
And secret, on this beautiful jewel throne,
Pray place your radiant feet firmly and grant us,
Who seek the supreme, all desired siddhi!

Blow the thighbone trumpet three times.

The offering of Ganachakra

HO! Blessed by samadhi, mantra, and mudra,
This ocean of offerings, feast of stainless nectar,
We offer to please you, hosts of root and lineage Gurus!

Play the damaru below in MA-DANG-KA-DRO rhythm:

OM AH HUM Satisfied, enjoying glory of all desirables,
EH MA HO Please let fall a great rain of blessings!

HO! Blessed by samadhi, mantra, and mudra,
This ocean of offerings, feast of stainless nectar,
We offer to please you, hosts of Yidams with your entourages!
OM AH HUM Satisfied, enjoying glory of all desirables,
EH MA HO Please let fall a great rain of attainments!

HO! Blessed by samadhi, mantra, and mudra,
This ocean of offerings, feast of stainless nectar,

We offer to please you, hosts of precious Jewels of Refuge!
OM AH HUM Satisfied, enjoying glory of all desirables,
EH MA HO Please let fall great rain of holy Dharma!

HO! Blessed by samadhi, mantra, and mudra
This ocean of offerings, feast of stainless nectar,
We offer to please you, hosts of Dakinis and Guardians!
OM AH HUM Satisfied, enjoying glory of all desirables,
EH MA HO Please let fall a great rain of activity!

HO! Blessed by samadhi, mantra, and mudra
This ocean of offerings, feast of stainless nectar,
We offer to please you, hosts of sentient beings, our mothers!
OM AH HUM Satisfied, enjoying glory of all desirables,
EH MA HO May hallucinated suffering be quelled!   (3x)

Make outer and inner offerings, reciting:

OM GURU BUDDHA BODHISATTVA DHARMAPALA
SAPARIWARA ARGHAM PADYAM PUPE DHUPE ALOKE
GHANDE NAIVIDYE SHABTA PRATICHA HUM SVAHA

OM GURU BUDDHA BODHISATTVA DHARMAPALA
SAPARIWARA OM AH HUM

Praise of Vajrayogini

OM Homage, Bhagavati Vajravarahi HUM HUM PHAT
OM Arya Wisdom Queen, by three realms, unchallenged HUM HUM
    PHAT
OM Conquering all fear of demons with great vajra HUM HUM
    PHAT
OM Vajra seat, unchallenged, with eyes of power HUM HUM PHAT
OM Tummo, in her furious form, melts Brahma HUM HUM PHAT
OM Cowing, crushing demons, all victorious HUM HUM PHAT

OM Conquering all who dull, stupefy, or confuse HUM HUM PHAT
OM Homage, wish-fulfilling Vajravarahi HUM HUM PHAT

The action vajras prostrate, then, holding the Ganachakra offerings, recite:

EH MA HO The great Ganachakra,
Path of three times' Sugatas,
Source of all attainments,
Knowing it thus, great hero,
Abandoning conceptions,
Always delight in Ganachakra!

A LA LA HO

The assembly recites:

OM Self generated as Guru Deva,
Inseparable three vajra nature,
AH this unstained wisdom nectar,
HUM Unmoving from bodhichitta,
I enjoy to satisfy the
Deities staying in my body!

AH HO MAHA SUKHA HO

Then, if done elaborately:

Prayer to See the Beautiful Face of the Dakini

Endless Buddhas' bliss-void dance rising
As any worldly or nirvanic sight,
Here, now, charming powerful Dakini,
Take me, who long for you, in embrace!

Pure Lands' innate Mother of Buddhas,
Twenty-four sites' field-born Dakinis,

All over the earth, Karmamudra,
Lady, my, the yogi's, supreme Refuge!

You are empty sport of essence mind,
In Vajra City, true BAM of E's sphere,
In world of illusion, appear as
Frightful rakshasas and vivacious maids.

Yet, where'er I searched, Arya Lady,
I could not find you truly existent.
Tired of projections, the youth of mind
Rested in the ineffable forest hut.

E MA! Now arise from Dakinis' sphere,
As Shri Heruka, King of Tantras, states,
"One attains by reading the Vajra Queen's
Great near-essence mantra"; uphold its truth!

In Odibisha's forested outskirts,
Lord of Siddhas, Vajra Ghantapa,
You cared for with bliss of kiss, embrace and
Enjoyed supreme union; care for me so!

As, from Ganges, Reverend Kusali
You took directly into the sky,
And cared for the glorious Naropa,
Lead me to blissful Dakiniland!

By the supreme Gurus' compassion,
This vast, most secret, deepest swift path, and
Pure wish to enlighten beings myself,
Soon may I see Dakini's smiling face!

Venerable Guru Vajrayogini, please guide me and all sentient beings to the
Pure Land of Dakinis! Please bestow on us every mundane and supramundane siddhi! (3x)

Next follows the "Song of the Spring Queen." Play the damaru in DRUM-DRUM and CHOM-DEN-DE rhythms. Then, if you wish, add special prayers, such as for long life of the Gurus, protection, and so forth. Then offer the remainder Ganachakra:

HUM All the Tathagatas and
Viras and Yoginis,
Dakas and Dakinis,
To you all, I make requests!
Heruka, who's pleased with supreme bliss,
In the bliss-crazed Lady delighting,
Enjoying, according to the rite,
Enters union of the innate bliss!
A LA LA, LA LA HO, AH EE AH HA AH RA LI HO
Hosts of stainless Dakinis,
Look with love and grant all feats.

HUM All the Tathagatas and
Viras and Yoginis,
Dakas and Dakinis,
To you all, I make requests!
Since the mind's excited by great bliss,
Body moves in vibrant dance, and thus,
Bliss felt in Mudra's lotus, let us
Offer to the hosts of Dakinis!
A LA LA, LA LA HO, AH EE AH HA AH RA LI HO
Hosts of stainless Dakinis,
Look with love and grant all feats.

HUM All the Tathagatas and
Viras and Yoginis,
Dakas and Dakinis,
To you all, I make requests!
Dear Mother whose dance expresses peace,
Blissful Lord, you and Dakini hosts,
Abiding before me, bless me and,

Upon me bestow innate great bliss!
A LA LA, LA LA HO, AH EE AH HA AH RA LI HO
Hosts of stainless Dakinis,
Look with love and grant all feats.

HUM All the Tathagatas and
Viras and Yoginis,
Dakas and Dakinis,
To you all, I make requests!
That great bliss with freedom's qualities
Abandoned, though gone through much hardship,
There's no release in one life, that bliss,
'Midst the supreme lotus, there abides!
A LA LA, LA LA HO, AH EE AH HA AH RA LI HO
Hosts of stainless Dakinis,
Look with love and grant all feats.

HUM All the Tathagatas and
Viras and Yoginis,
Dakas and Dakinis,
To you all, I make requests!
Like a lotus, born amidst a swamp,
From desire born, yet by it unstained,
By supreme Yogini's lotus bliss,
Swiftly free me from samsara's bonds!
A LA LA, LA LA HO, AH EE AH HA AH RA LI HO
Hosts of stainless Dakinis,
Look with love and grant all feats.

HUM All the Tathagatas and
Viras and Yoginis,
Dakas and Dakinis,
To you all, I make requests!
Just as swarms of bees drink their fill of
Honey's essence from the flowers' source,

May I, by Ishvari's full lotus,
By taste bound with essence, be fulfilled!
A LA LA, LA LA HO, AH EE AH HA AH RA LI HO
Hosts of stainless Dakinis,
Look with love and grant all feats.

HUM Impure illusions are purified in emptiness's sphere
AH This great nectar of transcendent wisdom,
OM Becomes a vast ocean of all desirable.

OM AH HUM (3x)

HO! Blessed by samadhi, mantra, and mudra
This ocean of remaining feast of stainless nectar,
We offer to please you hosts of oath-bound realm protectors.
OM AH HUM Satisfied, enjoying glory of all desirables,
EH MA HO Well perform the yogi's activities!

O guests for the remainder and entourage,
Having received this ocean of leftovers from the feast,
Spread the precious Teachings, and,
For upholders of the Teachings, their entourage,
And especially for us, the yogis,
Grant long life without illness, power,
Glory, renown, good fortune,
And full attainment of vast prosperity!
Grant us attainment of activities
Such as pacification and increase!
Avowed guardians, protect us!
Grant help in all attainments!
Eliminate untimely death, disease,
Spirits and obstructers,
Bad dreams, omens and activities!
May the world be at peace, crops be good,
May harvests increase, and Dharma flourish!

May all happiness and goodness manifest,
And may all our wishes be fulfilled!

By force of this vast generosity
May I become Buddha, myself, for the sake of all,
And may multitudes not freed by past Buddhas,
By this generosity, be freed!

[*Additional dedication verses recited without damaru in Kyabje Zong Rinpoche's
oral tradition:*

Whatever spirits are still left here,
Whether dwelling on the earth or in the sky,
May I always have great love for them,
And may they all enjoy the Dharma day and night!

If the smallest virtue is dedicated with supreme skillful means of the
    Bodhisattva's prayer,
The smallest seed attains to excellence and quickly becomes inexhaustible.
To transform every virtue of the three times into great waves of prayer,
Who with intelligence would not make effort with these skillful means?

Connected with every collection of goodness
Of the past, present, or future,
Source of all attainments and the supreme,
May I have devotion for the holy Spiritual Guide!

In the ship of the fully endowed human form,
Flying the white sail of mindfulness of impermanence,
Blown by the wind of adopting and abandoning in accordance with
    cause and effect,
May I be freed from the fearsome ocean of cyclic existence!

Devoting myself to the crown jewel of the nonfallacious objects of refuge,
Taking to heart the great aims of living beings who have all been my mother,

And cleansing myself of all stains of faults with the nectar of Vajrasattva,
May I be nurtured by the compassion of the Venerable Gurus!

The beautiful motherly consort of the Victorious Buddhas is the outer
    Yogini,
The syllable BAM is the supreme inner Vajra Queen,
The voidness clarity that is the very nature of mind itself is the secret
    Mother from Dakiniland;
May I enjoy the playful bliss of seeing these, your faces!

The worldly environment is the celestial mansion coming from the
    syllables EH EH,
The sentient beings within are Yoginis coming from the syllable BAM
Through single-minded concentration on the great bliss of their unity,
May whatever appearances I see arise as pure appearance!

Thus, through the yogas numbering as many as the ten directions and
    the single moon,
May I eventually be led directly to the City of Knowledge Holders
By the coral-colored Lady of Bliss,
With freely hanging vermillion hair and orange darting eyes!

Having practiced in the corpse-laden place with trunk of sindhura-filled
    langali tree,
And then wandered searching throughout all the lands,
May whichever beautiful lady to whom the bliss swirl
At my forehead transfers lead me to Dakiniland!

When the inner Varahi has destroyed the creeping vine of my precon-
    ceptions,
About grasping consciousness and the objects it grasps,
And the dancing Lady residing in my supreme central channel emerges
    from the aperture of Brahma into the sphere of the pathway of the
    clouds,
May I embrace and sport with the Vira-hero Drinker of Blood!

At my death may Heruka, the Heroes and Heroines,
Escort me holding flowers, parasols, and victory banners,
And offering music of cymbals, lutes, and so forth,
Guide me to the Pure Land of Dakinis!

May the truth of the valid Goddesses,
Their valid commitments,
And the supremely valid words they have spoken
Become the cause for us to be cared for by the Goddesses!

The hundred-syllable mantra of Vajrasattva is then recited with bell.]

Done elaborately, giving of Dharma may be performed here playing damaru with
DRUM-DRUM and CHOM-DEN-DE rhythms. Then recite:[110]

Thus offered, all enjoy stainless bliss!
Beings attain unobscured Dharmakaya!
The offering's three spheres become nondual
Bliss-void, beyond speech, thought or expression!

PHAT
Giving's three spheres are just labeled names and sounds
And exist, not even an atom, from their side,
Though living and inanimate things appear to
Exist truly, they're empty, like illusions.

PHAT PHAT PHAT

All appearances gather, as light, into my heart,
And I abide in yoga of spacelike emptiness.
Spacelike experience of objectless emptiness,
With understanding of emptiness of inherent existence.

Gathering all appearances into light and into your heart, meditate on spacelike empti-
ness with the two or four points, the two being (1) the appearance being clear and empty,

*and (2) the understanding being strong ascertainment of emptiness of inherent exis-
tence.*[111] *After meditating, make brief or extensive prayers of dedication. In brief:*

PHAT
Though things' natures are free of projections,
Various emanated conventions appear.
EVAM's union of wisdom-means, may it bring
Truth and form bodies, free of obscuration!

Buddha, supreme of the great, unexcelled,
Through Buddha, the Sun Lord of Dharma's blessings
Calming the foe, maras and hinderers; may night and
Day be always glorious and auspicious!

Dharma, supreme, sublime truth, unexcelled,
Through holy Dharma amrita's blessing,
Calming the foe, tormenting delusions; may night and
Day be always glorious and auspicious!

Sangha's precious qualities blazing, through Bodhisattvas'
Beneficial deeds' truth's blessings,
Increasing virtuous collections, faultless; may night and
Day be always glorious and auspicious!

*This was compiled by Venerable Vajradhara Zong Rinpoche Losang Tsöndru for easy
recitation.*

> *May all sentient beings as vast as space,*
> *Be cared for by supreme Gurus, and,*
> *Ripened through the three principal paths,*
> *Attain the glorious state free of self-cherishing!*

Umapa Pawo Dorje's Commentary on Chöd as Taught by Venerable Manjushri

Homage to the Guru and Venerable Vajrayogini!

This Chöd is taught in three points: the preliminaries, the actual practice, and the concluding section, the uprisings and resolutions.

PRELIMINARIES

The first of the three preliminaries is Guru Yoga. At your crown or heart, visualize an eight-petal lotus upon which is your Guru, inseparable from the Venerable Lady; make requests.

The second is Vajrasattva meditation and mantra recitation. As in the scripture, visualizing Vajrasattva at your crown, reciting the hundred-syllable mantra, contemplate all negativity and obscuration being purified.

The third is mandala offering. Visualize your own mind, inseparable from Venerable Machig, rising up out of your crown, skinning your body. Upon the spread-out skin, in the center are placed your head and heart; in the four directions, your four limbs; in the intermediate directions, your intestines, and so forth. Visualize these as the powerful golden ground upon which is Mount Sumeru made of jewels, the four continents, sun, moon and so forth, which you offer repeatedly to the Guru and Three Jewels.

The Actual Practice

This includes eight visualizations.

First, having generated yourself as Vajrayogini, make requests to the Guru and Three Jewels, meditate on love, compassion and bodhichitta, meditate on impermanence and death again and again, and, in particular, contemplate from the depths of your heart that, in order for all sentient beings to attain enlightenment, "I shall offer this body to the buddhas and bodhisattvas, dharmapalas and dakas and dakinis, and give it to sentient beings." Know how to apply these contemplations appropriately in all the visualizations.

Visualize the Venerable Lady inseparable from your own mind, emerging from your crown, cutting off your crown with her curved knife, placing it on a tripod of three human heads before her, and putting all the flesh and blood inside it. Wind stirs from below and the fire blazes, heating the skullcup. Reciting OM AH HUM three times, visualize it melting into light and becoming an inconceivable ganachakra of wisdom nectar. Visualize to the fore an ornate celestial palace, in the center of which, on a lion-supported jewel throne, is your root Guru in the aspect of Vajradhara. Visualize the Guru surrounded by an inconceivable host of gurus, yidams, buddhas and bodhisattvas in sambhogakaya aspect. Contemplate emanating countless Venerable Ladies inseparable from your own mind, each holding a skullcup in both hands, with which they serve the guests, and from which the guests partake, beginning with Vajradhara, delighting and satisfying them all. Request the fulfillment of all temporary and ultimate aims. From OM at Vajradhara's crown come white rays of light, dissolving into the point between your eyebrows, purifying physical negativity, and you receive the vase empowerment. From AH at his throat come red rays of light, dissolving into your throat, purifying vocal negativity, and you receive the secret empowerment. From HUM at his heart come blue rays of light, dissolving into your heart, purifying mental negativity, and you receive the *prajnajnana* initiation. From the three syllables come multicolored rays of light, dissolving into all of your places, purifying negativity, and you receive the fourth initiation.

Second, having offered to the host of dharmapala guardians visualized as before, request activities pacifying all conditions obstructive to Dharma practice and providing the conditions conducive to effortless accomplishment.

Third, contemplate giving to the six realms' sentient beings meditated on as being your parents as before. This generosity is to repay their kindness to you.

Fourth, give to satisfy the desires of sentient beings seen as being in a pitiful state.

Fifth, give to all sentient beings to repay your karmic debts to them.

Sixth, give the body of flesh and blood actually visualized as such to all worldly, malicious beings who like flesh and blood.

In the remaining visualizations recite as follows:

Eighty thousand types of obstructers in the world, fifteen great demons harmful to infants, lords of disease, lords of plagues, devas, goddesses, and rakshasas of the eight classes and so forth, all of you who want flesh, eat flesh! Those who want blood, drink blood! Likewise, those who want bones, outer flesh or inner organs, limbs, juices and so forth, take them as you wish!

Giving it all, visualizing the flesh and blood as extensive as space, contemplate all being satisfied. Do this Chöd visualization four times every day. The four times are evening twilight, first light, sunrise, and sunset. From the second visualization onward, also recite:

Separate my mind and body! Set all disease upon me! Especially beset me with leprosy, cancer, and boils! Give my body as food to malicious demons and obstructers! As I am giving you my body in order to purify all karmic debts to sentient beings, all bad karma and ripening effects, do not harm any other sentient being, and take this body of mine right now!

Say this repeatedly.

Seventh, generate all demons and obstructers in the middle of the flesh and blood, and do as before.

Eighth, contemplate wrathful deities in the ten directions, summoning all the demons and obstructers to the center of the flesh and blood in the midst of a great wisdom fire, and, with them forced to remain there without choice, do as before.

Finally, attend to all sorts of nonhuman spirits. Then, collect all into yourself. You must then abide in profound completion stage practice; or, lacking that, you must be able to attain stability in another virtuous application, and it is very important that it be sustained by the two bodhichittas. As this practice is done for the sake of severing the root of self and so forth, do not bring harm to others through such actions as digging up earth, turning over boulders, cutting down trees or bushes, disturbing water, or disturbing spirits of the land and so forth. Yet, you should give your body in this instance, because it is done in order to help sever your self-grasping ignorance, to train in the visualizations, and, furthermore, to abandon views of self-existence, to take the negative karma of all beings upon yourself, to purify all their negative karma and karmic debts that you owe to them, and in order for them to attain enlightenment. In particular, for setting malicious beings into the state of enlightenment, this skillful means is indispensable. Abandon aversion to disease and wanting to be free of illness, because it is very important to give up self-grasping ignorance in all circumstances. Meditate perceiving as pleasurable whatever bad conditions occur, because, without incorporating them into the path, it is impossible to train in Chöd.

UPRISINGS AND RESOLUTIONS

Thirdly, the concluding section has two parts: the uprisings and their resolutions.

As to the first, there is the matter of the site, and then the actual nature of the uprisings. The means to extensively examine the sites where beings such as malicious devas or nagas abide is similar in other contexts. It is said that you should go secretly to disagreeable places. After some time, you can go wherever you wish, and you should go unbeknownst to anyone. Don't even tell anyone where you are going. As soon as you arrive, stack marker stones in the four directions. Generate the site as a mandala mansion on a crossed vajra, and yourself as the yidam deity within it. Around the circumference, make a fence of mustard seeds, and meditate on a vast surrounding protection wheel. Be aware that this is a means to prevent both yourself and others from leaving. Then, give a white torma to the landowners of the site, and command them:

> I am dedicating this to you with the aim of benefiting others at this site, so grant me your aid!

Then engage in the practice with the visualizations.

Next, as to the nature of the disturbing uprisings, there are two types: inner uprisings and outer uprisings.

The first ones are occurrences such as feeling unhappy, feeling afraid, wanting to leave, not wanting to engage in virtuous practice, sudden arising of the afflictive emotions, and various types of displeasure.

Outer uprisings are—in actuality or in dreams—the occurrence of being carried off in water, burned in fire, blown by wind, the earth splitting, being squeezed between mountains, vicious wild animals, and malicious sentient beings, human or nonhuman, creating inconceivable manifestations. Uprising-like resolutions are such that, once the uprising has occurred, that very manifestation then bows respectfully to you and requests Dharma, or some such pleasant aspect then appears. Resolution-like uprisings are such that, although the manifestation bows with respect at first, it then reveals an unpleasant, disturbing aspect. Simultaneous uprising-resolutions are such that an unpleasant aspect is revealed at the beginning but, daily, you give instructions to it, and it bows respectfully to you.

As for resolutions, they are of two types: inner resolutions and outer resolutions.

Inner resolutions are the fresh arising of many spiritual qualities within oneself, such as compassion, faith, renunciation, or total absence of self-grasping ignorance.

Outer resolutions are displays of pleasant aspects by nonhuman spirits and so forth, in actuality or in dreams, venerating and serving you, making offerings and praises, or attending to Dharma teachings. It sometimes happens that nonhuman spirits, in order to create obstructions, display resolution-type appearances, so you should not be satisfied with just a few resolutions. Some nonhuman spirits, after showing some disturbing uprising, are unable to demonstrate resolution, and some are not subdued by the visualizations without showing either uprising or resolution. Therefore, if by performing, one after the other, with stable visualization, the four visualizations from the fifth to the eighth, no uprising whatsoever occurs, the spirits are unable to reveal uprisings and resolutions even though they are there. If it is a place where powerful spirits are, in fact, abiding, you should remain performing the visualizations until uprisings and resolutions do occur. If you are unable to subdue a malicious deva or ghost through the visualizations and there is no uprising whatsoever, you should perform a ritual to move them on. To do that, generate refuge and bodhichitta and, in particular, compassion and bodhichitta focused on that spirit especially, and do the visualizations over and over again with the intention to subdue it and set that very spirit into the state of enlightenment. Then, from within emptiness, meditate that you arise on a sun cushion as the Venerable Lady, within a blazing fire of transcendent wisdom. Visualize yourself with an entourage of innumerable male and female wrathful deities having all the outfits and implements of wrathful ones, and emanate countless male and female wrathful deities from your heart. Visualize that spirit itself in the form of a fierce animal, such as a tiger or leopard that the yidam deities lasso and catch with hooks. Having tied it up in chains, it is summoned and brought forth without any choice, and cooked in the wisdom fire. Contemplate that the yidams eat it, liberating it, and that its consciousness also becomes nondual with the wisdom minds of the yidam deities. Then collect all of the deities into yourself. Contemplate that you also disappear like a rainbow into space, and remain in completion stage meditation, or, lacking that, simply remain completely absent, like a rainbow that has disappeared. Then continue doing any of the last four Chöd visualizations you wish. This ritual for moving a spirit on should not, however, be performed by someone with impure samaya, someone without attainment of stability in generation or completion stage meditation, or someone whose sense of the true existence of self is too strong.

Then, if resolution is complete and you are soon going to move on, such as in the morning of the next day, that evening before dark, having given a torma to the land-owners, say that you are staying five or six more days, and command them to grant assistance. When you are about to leave, request the protection wheel and boundary stone mandala to be dismissed, and leave nothing of your own behind. Then, go a number of steps, perhaps twenty-one or so, in a direction other than that in which you actually intend to go, and then turn your shoes around backwards, toes to your heel, and take your actual route. Having gone a number of steps, such as twenty-one, or once you arrive at a crossroads, a cliff, or a hill, make a design of a crossed vajra there and generate it as a protection wheel with the mountain of fire around it, but generate no deity within. Then, maintaining virtuous practice, move on without even glancing back. Arriving back at your retreat hut, without having been distracted, you should remain several days in virtuous practice.

As for those who lack familiarity with these points involved in examining a site, if their visualizations have not subdued the spirits, although they may know some sort of site analysis, they will not accomplish the actual purpose of their practice. Even if they know visualizations and points of the instructions, no matter where they do the practice, and no matter what arisings and resolutions they claim have occurred, they have not accurately assessed the signs at the site.

This Chöd commentary has been prepared by Pawo Dorje according to the teaching of Venerable Manjushri.

Prayer for the Flourishing of Je Tsongkhapa's Teachings

BY GUNGTHANG TENPAI DRONME

Though Father from whom all Conquerors are born,
You vowed to uphold the Conqueror's Dharma
As a Bodhisattva in infinite worlds; through that truth's power,
May Conqueror Losang's Teachings flourish.

When, previously, before Buddha Indraketu,
You made your vow, the Conqueror and Bodhisattvas
Praised your great courage; through that truth's power,
May Conqueror Losang's Teachings flourish.

That pure view and action's lineage might flourish
You offered crystal mala before Shakyamuni,
Who gave you white conch and prophecy; through that truth's power
May Conqueror Losang's Teachings flourish.

Pure view free from permanence and nihilism's extremes,
Pure meditation cleared of laxity's foggy gloom,
Pure action according with the Conqueror's speech,
May Conqueror Losang's Teachings flourish.

Wisdom through having extensively sought Teachings,
Purity through applying their meaning to oneself,

Kindness through dedicating it all for Dharma and beings,
May Conqueror Losang's Teachings flourish.

Cessation of all faulty conduct through gaining
Certainty that all scriptures, definitive and interpretive,
Are, without contradiction, advice for one person's practice,
May Conqueror Losang's Teachings flourish.

Through hearing three Pitakas, the scriptural Dharma,
And practicing three trainings, the realized Teachings,
Living an exalted life of mastery and attainment,
May Conqueror Losang's Teachings flourish.

Outwardly, Shravaka's conduct, serene and subdued,
Internally, confident in yoga's two stages,
Sutra and tantra's excellent paths, not contradictory, but complementary,
May Conqueror Losang's Teachings flourish.

Emptiness as explained through the causal vehicle,
And great bliss achieved through the resultant one's means,
In union, eighty-four thousand Teaching collections' nectar essence,
May Conqueror Losang's Teachings flourish.

Through power of an ocean of the Teachings' sworn Guardians,
Such as the three scopes' paths' principal Protectors,
Swift Mahakala, Vaishravana and Kalarupa,
May Conqueror Losang's Teachings flourish.

In short, the glorious Gurus' lives firmly stable,
Pure wise sublime bearers of the Teachings all over the earth,
Through the Teachings' patrons' dominions spreading,
May Conqueror Losang's Teachings flourish.

The Sages' Melodious Song of Truth: Nonpartisan Prayer for the Flourishing of Buddha's Teachings

BY HIS HOLINESS THE FOURTEENTH DALAI LAMA

Omniscient Sun Friend Buddha, four Kayas in nature,
Supreme Aryas Amitayus, Amitabha, Avalokiteshvara,
Manjushri, Vajrapani, Tara, Wrathful Ones,
Hosts of Great Beings, Buddhas, Bodhisattvas,

Seven Great Hierarchs, Six Ornaments, Two Supreme Ones,
Eighty-four Mahasiddhas, Sixteen Arhats, and so forth,
Who've shouldered responsibility to benefit beings and the Teachings,
Hosts of supreme great Beings, please listen to me!

By the truth that the Supreme Able One, over countless eons,
Fully completed the two accumulations of merit and wisdom,
Thus perfecting wisdom, compassion and power,
May the whole of Buddha's Teachings forever flourish!

Doors through whom Buddha's Teachings first illumined the
   Land of Snows,
Padmasambhava, Shantarakshita and Trisong Deutsen,
Translators, Pandits, Tantrikas, the Master and major disciples,
By power of your Bodhichitta, may Buddhism of the Land of Snows
   forever flourish!

In an arbor of jewels of the vast Teachings,
Profound Practice School of the great Termas of Dharma,
The brilliant sharp light of the super profound Heart Drop,
May Buddhism of the Land of Snows forever flourish!

Great expanse of essence, primordially pure clear light in which
All phenomena, samsara and beyond, are comprehensively Perfected,
Supreme of Vehicles to the Kingdom of innate Samantabhadra,
May Buddhism of the Land of Snows forever flourish!

Lineages of profound view and vast conduct coming
Through Atisha, he endowed with treasury of all the precepts,
And Drom Tönpa Gyalwa Jungne, this system of instructions,
May Buddhism of the Land of Snows forever flourish!

Well incorporating all Buddha's Teachings comprised in the three
    Pitakas,
In instructions suited to beings of initial, intermediate and advanced
    capacity,
The sevenfold Deity and Dharma Practice of the golden garland
    of Kadampas,
May Buddhism of the Land of Snows forever flourish!

Marpa the Translator, Laughing Vajra Milarepa, and so on,
Treasure mine of the Kagyu, source of blessings,
The unique Dharma system of this incomparable lineage,
May Buddhism of the Land of Snows forever flourish!

Realizing all samsara and nirvana to be innate mind's reflection,
Mind essence free of projection to be Dharmakaya,
Mahamudra encompassing all existence, samsara and beyond,
May Buddhism of the Land of Snows forever flourish!

Protecting Buddhadharma through writing, teaching, and debate,
Of the vast scriptures of Sutra and Tantra, outer and inner fields,

Masters of the divine Kön lineage, the sublime Sakya,
May Buddhism of the Land of Snows forever flourish!

The ear-whispered lineage endowed with four valid perceptions,
And extremely profound essential points of the Path and Fruits
    practice,
The system of instructions of the Sakyas, such Lords of Yogis,
May Buddhism of the Land of Snows forever flourish!

Profound Madhyamika view closely coupled
With the great secrets of Vajrayana's two stages,
Masterfully illumined to their depths and propagated, Conqueror
    Losang's Teachings,
May Buddhism of the Land of Snows forever flourish!

This supreme excellent path of unmistaken practice,
Of the Stages of the Path to Enlightenment incorporating
The entirety of the three Pitakas and four classes of Tantra,
May Buddhism of the Land of Snows forever flourish!

Its approach differing from other Sutras and Tantras,
Outer, inner and alternative Kalachakra, Wheel of Time,
Transmission and realizations of the Butön and Jonang lineages,
May Buddhism of the Land of Snows forever flourish!

In brief, rich with many instructions unifying Sutra and Tantra,
Exposition of the ten great treatises of study,
A chariot of practice for all, Dampa's Pacifier tradition, and so forth,
May Buddhism of the Land of Snows forever flourish!

May Dharma's upholders live long, may Sangha be in harmony
And cultivate the three turnings of the Wheel of Dharma!
May earth be pervaded by those with faith in Dharma,
And the Teachings, without partisanship, flourish forever!

May not even the words "conflict, war, starvation,
Evil acts or intentions" be heard in this world!
May love, awareness, and good flourish in beings and the environment,
And all realms be filled with oceans of happiness!

May I, as well, henceforth strive in focused study and meditation
On the complete path of the Teachings'
Vast bodhichitta and profound view,
And soon attain state of all temporal and ultimate well-being!

For the sake of sentient beings to the very ends of space,
May I engage in that conduct of the Buddhas and Bodhisattvas,
Without any discouragement, attachment, or laziness,
But with deep conviction, sincere aspiration and joy!

May my body, wealth, and virtues,
Become a cause for mother sentient beings' happiness,
And may all of their misery and suffering
Ripen on me without remainder!

May all those who see, hear, remember, or admire me,
Each, as well, enjoy blissful happiness,
Free from physical and mental abuse,
And have good fortune to be on the path to enlightenment!

In brief, for as long as space exists,
And as long as suffering of beings persists,
For that long, may I remain, to become
Whatever, directly or indirectly, benefits beings!

In regard to these Teachings of the Infinitely Compassionate One who, while seeing all conventional and ultimate phenomena to be like illusions, manifests enlightening activities throughout space, the Founder Lord Buddha's complete Teachings of Lesser and Greater Vehicles including Tantra, this most cherished jewel of Dharma of the Land of Snow, thinking that it would be good if there was a nonpartisan prayer indicating how each of the Great Dharma Masters who have accomplished powerful prayers to uphold holy Buddhadharma have sustained, protected, and propitiated the different lineages of Tibet's precious Buddhist Teachings so that in these latter times general and individual trainees' glory of merit may not decline, and so that all of the lineages may flourish for a long time; and urged to compose it by the twelfth incarnation of Padampa, Chusang Rinpoche Trinle Gyatso, and other faithful aspirants, and in particular, urged to compose it by one who perseveres in the nonpartisan Teachings that illumine the early Teachings, the great sustainer, protector, and propitiator of the Vinaya which survived from lower Do Kham in lineage from the great Guru Gongpa Rabsel, Tzarong Shwadeu Trulshig Ngawang Chökyi Lodrö Rinpoche, I, the Shakya monk Tenzin Gyatso, having understood and attained faith in Buddha's Teachings, and having attained pure view, aspiration, and devotion for the Rime, nonpartisan, Buddhadharma, strongly striving to study and meditate on them, wrote this in the year generally accepted as 2543 years after Buddha's Parinirvana, the Tibetan year 2126, seventeenth twelve-year cycle, thirteenth of the first month of the Year of the Earth Hare, day of February 24, 1999, in India, Land of the Aryas, state of Himachal Pradesh, Kangra Tzong, in Dharamsala at Tegchen Chöling. By the blessings of the Buddhas and Bodhisattvas may it be so accomplished!

Notes

1 Although his family lineage was Nyingma, Zong Rinpoche's incarnation lineage had been Gelug for a number of previous lifetimes.

2 A ceremonial offering of food by an assembly of Tantric practitioners called *tsog kyi korlo* (*tshogs kyi 'khor lo*) in Tibetan or *ganachakra* in Sanskrit.

3 Excerpt from a spontaneous song of realization. The complete song, as it is chanted in the context of ganachakra:

> Up in pure Keajra, Akanishta's realm,
> Beautiful maiden, graceful Mother of Conquerors,
> With a display of countless emanations,
> Acts as the fortunate's guide to Kechari.
>
> In the sixty-four "E sphere" Dakas' city,
> Supremely beautiful smiling Chandali,
> Agilely, playfully, dancing like lightning
> Enjoys sport of EVAM spontaneous with bliss.
>
> Mind 'midst the eight petals in avadhuti,
> Free of all projections, Clear Light's Bliss Goddess,
> Magical Lady of Five Lights' beautiful play
> Puts on a show of inconceivable Union!
>
> How pleasant, this profound, most secret swift path!
> How blissful, this gathering with pure samaya!
> In the glory of Ganachakra's blissful Union,
> This connection transcends meeting and parting!

4 The term "Ganden tradition" is synonymous here with "Gelug" and "Geden," except when Ganden Monastery is mentioned specifically. Ganden is often spelled *Gaden*, as well. The *n* in *Gaden* represents a nasalization in the Tibetan pronunciation, but there is no actual letter *n* in the Tibetan spelling of the word, which is *dGa' ldan*.

5 Tsongkhapa's *Commentary on the Profound Path of Chöd* is translated in Carol Diane Savvas, "A Study of the Profound Path of gCod" (PhD dissertation, University of Wisconsin, Madison, 1990), pp. 308-399.

6 Machig Labkyi Drölma or Machig Labdrön (1055- approx. 1153). She was prophesied by Buddha in the fifty-third chapter of the *Sutra Distinguishing the Pure and the Dregs* (Tib. *mDo sde dang snyigs 'byed pa*):

When conflict arises in degenerate times, in the Land of Snows to the north, Machig Labdrön, a manifestation of Mother Prajnaparamita, will appear.

Also in the *Root Tantra of Manjushri* (Skt. *Manjushrimulatantra,*Tib. *'Jam dpal rtsa brgyud*) Buddha prophesied,

During degenerate times of my teachings, in the city of Lab to the north, there will appear a manifestation of Buddha's wisdom teachings. Called by the name of Drönma, her teachings will flourish as she wanders in the mountains, caves, cemeteries, towns and cities and their outskirts, expounding the meaning of Emptiness.

When Maching Labdrön was sixteen, she was hosted for four years by a Geshe during which time she recited the entire long, medium, and short *Prajnaparamita Sutras*. While she was reading the *Chapter on Mara* from the medium-length *Twenty Thousand Verse Prajnaparamita Sutra* she came across the following passages:

All apprehension of independent existence in everything, from form to omniscience, is the work of mara.

Innately existent form does not come from anywhere, nor does it go anywhere, and it doesn't abide anywhere else.

All phenomena are equally void of inherent existence; thus the perfect wisdom "gone beyond" is also void of inherent existence.

Another passage that caught her attention was in the *Condensed Perfection of Wisdom Sutra* (Tib. *mDo bsdud pa*):

Even if sentient beings equal in number to the atoms of water in the river Ganges were to turn into maras and emanate maras from each of their pores equal to the number of atoms of water in the river Ganges, they would still be unable to hinder a person who has trained and meditated on emptiness.

Through pondering these passages she spontaneously attained realization of emptiness, severing the root of self-grasping mind. This became the foundation for her system of Chöd.

7 On the Dakini oral lineage, see note 48.

8 Janice D. Willis, *Enlightened Beings: Life Stories from the Ganden Oral Tradition* (Boston: Wisdom Publications, 1995), pp. 33-34.

9 His present incarnation, Zong Chogtrul Rinpoche Tenzin Wangdag Trinlé Gyaltsen, now attends Ganden Mahayana University, which has been reestablished in South India.

10 Wisdom stupa: see the biographical profile, pg. 00.

11 This was because Chöd was seen as taking time away from studies of the major treatises. Although Je Tsongkhapa's teachings are a union of Sutra and Tantra, the two are not always studied and practiced together. The extensive Sutra study done in the monasteries easily requires more than twenty years of undivided attention; on completion of Sutra studies, monks will frequently enter one of the Tantric colleges. As in all traditions of Tibetan Buddhism, a Gelugpa monk usually has some contact with Tantric practice from an early age, but this is pursued individually rather than as part of the monastic curriculum, particularly in the case of Sera and Drepung. The curriculum of Ganden Monastery is distinguished as being a union of Sutra and Tantra.

12 *King Giving of Instructions Sutra: mDo sde gdams ngag 'bogs pa'i rgyal po.*

13 Leaf-enwreathed pillar (*ka ba shing lo can*): a pillar in the Lhasa temple under which treasure of the Tibetan King Songtsen Gampo is said to be buried.

14 Forthcoming from Rudra Press (Portland, OR) as *Lion of Siddhas, The Life and Teachings of Padampa Sangye*. Translated by David Molk with Venerable Lama Wangdu Rinpoche. *Lion of Siddhas* incorporates two Tibetan texts: *The Life of Venerable Dampa Sangye, the Great Lord of Siddhas, entitled A Sun Blazing with Light of Attainment (Grub pa'i dbang phyug chen po rje btsun dam pa sangs rgyas kyi rnam par thar pa dngos sgrub 'od stong 'bar ba'i nyi ma)*, and *Three Rounds of Dampa Sangye's Teaching of Mahamudra in Symbols (Dam pa sangs rgyas kyi phyag rgya chen po brda'i gskor gsum)*.

15 Other great Tibetan lamas are renowned to be incarnations of Padampa Sangye, such as the Karmapas, Karma Pakshi, Rangjung Dorje, and Karmapa Mikyö Dorje. I am in no way disputing these or the identities of any other lamas. Indeed, I prefer to view our gurus as part of the same continuum, just as we have many of the same lineage gurus, and the same Teacher Buddha. The manifestations of the enlightened Gurus are completely unlimited and inconceivable; they can be multiple and simultaneous!

16 Padampa Sangye's brother Chandrakirti is said to have lived three hundred years.

17 For example, drawing from Khetsun Sangpo's oral teachings, Jeffrey Hopkins writes, "The founder of the Shi-jay order was Pa-dam-ba-sang-gyay, who many say was Bodhidharma, also known as Kamalashila…. He was a student of eighty gurus, including Nagarjuna, Maitripada, and Naropa, lived for over five hundred years, visited Tibet five times, spread Buddhism widely in both China and Tibet, and is said to have visited Mi-la-re-ba near the end of his life. Based on the Perfection of Wisdom Sutras, he divided his teaching into three systems—sutra, tantra, and union of sutra and tantra—spreading a doctrine much like that of sudden enlightenment. It is said that he pretended to die a few times in China." *Meditation on Emptiness* (London: Wisdom Publications, 1983), pp. 536-37.

18 From *Lion of Siddhas* (see note 14).

19 The source for this is *Liberation in Our Hands*. Perhaps the meeting that took place at Nyanang Tongla between Padampa Sangye and Milarepa was a play of the same enlightened mind. At one point in the course of their interaction Padampa tells Milarepa, "Among Tibetan practitioners, to find one who is unfabricated, here *you* are! Even in India there are no more than one or two like you!"

20 An alternative oral tradition in the monastery has it that Kyabje Zong Rinpoche was Khedrubje.

21 *Lamp Illuminating the Ritual Practice of the Chöd Scripture: Guide for Those Seeking Liberation (gCod gzhung thar 'dod ded dpon ma'i cho ga don gsal bar ston pa'i nyams len gsal ba'i sgron me)*, by Drubwang Losang Namgyal.

22 Even though, at times, in the inconceivable displays of enlightenment, the same enlightened mind can manifest in multiple, simultaneous emanations that appear to be at odds with each other. The reason for this is to draw out and demonstrate the greatness of the enlightened beings, similar to the way that Devadatta, an emanation of Indra from the definitive point of view, drew out and demonstrated Buddha Shakyamuni's greatness.

23 Shijay (*zhi byed*): Padampa Sangye's Pacification of Suffering tradition.

24 *Four Songs to Je Rinpoche,* translated by Glenn Mullin with Lozang Tsonawa (Dharamsala, India: The Library of Tibetan Works and Archives, 1978).

25 From *Lion of Siddhas* (see note 14).

26 It is maintained that even to realize emptiness when subtlest clear light mind is mani-

festing, a subtle form of this insight must be sustained, because otherwise beings would attain liberation whenever they experienced the clear light of sleep!

27 Krishnapada was one of Padampa Sangye's fifty-four male and female mahasiddha gurus whose instructions he brought to Tibet. Padampa Sangye passed on this precept from Krishnapada:

> Setting the bird of rigpa wisdom aflight through the gazes, energies of deception can no longer predominate, causing realization of clear light, free of coming and going! This is the instruction of Krishnapada.

Padampa Sangye introduced disciples to the clear light nature of their own mind. Taking primordial, elemental mind as the primary object of meditation, in connection with the use of specific types of gazes and various mantras, he taught how to transmute the five poisons into the five transcendent wisdoms: by facing them directly and seeing their unborn nature.

28 Another oral tradition asserts that he was Je Tsongkhapa.

29 After recording my English musical translation of *Kadro Gekyang, the Jigme Lingpa Chöd, Laughter of the Dakinis* for one of Chusang Rinpoche's disciples, Rinpoche gave me the Tibetan text of this prayer for the flourishing of all schools of Tibetan Buddhism. It was he who requested its composition by His Holiness the Fourteenth Dalai Lama. Venerable Chusang Rinpoche, of the Kagyu tradition, is considered to be an incarnation of Padampa Sangye.

30 Prajnaparamita, in Tibetan *shes rab kyi pha rol tu phyin pa*: transcendent wisdom, sixth of the bodhisattvas' perfections, as taught by Buddha in the extensive, middling, and brief versions of the Perfection of Wisdom sutras. These Mahayana sutras are referred to as the "Mother" sutras, as realization of this wisdom gives birth to the attainments of all vehicles. The Great Mother Prajnaparamita also personifies this wisdom in the aspect of a yidam deity.

31 Bodhichitta: the altruistic aspiration to enlightenment.

32 Je Tsongkhapa Losang Dragpa (1357-1419), also known as Je Rinpoche.

33 The three vajra brothers: Dharmavajra, Drubchen Chökyi Dorje (no dates are given because he is said to have attained the siddhi of immortality); Gwalwa Ensapa, Ensa Losang Dondrub (1505-1565); and Sangye Yeshe (1525-1591).

34 An extensive listing of the Panchen Lama incarnations begins with four Indian incarnations: Subhuti, Shri Manjushrikirti, Lekden Je, and Abhayakaragupta. The Tibetan incarnations are recognized as Gö Lotsawa Kukpa Hletse, Sakya Pandita Kunga Gyaltsen, Yungtön Dorje Pel, Khedrub Je, Sönam Choglang, and Gyalwa Ensapa, prior to those counted as the first two Panchen Lamas.

35 *Chöd Instruction Guide for Those Seeking Liberation: Tardö Depön (gCod kyi gdams pa thar 'dod ded dpon)*.

36 Tsechog Ling Yongdzin Yeshe Gyaltsen (1713-1793).

37 *Lamp Illuminating the Ritual Practice of the Chöd Scripture: Guide for Those Seeking Liberation (gCod gzhung thar 'dod ded dpon ma'i cho ga don gsal bar ston pa'i nyams len gsal ba'i sgron me)*, by Drubwang Losang Namgyal.

38 *Ornament Illuminating the Intention of the Chöd Scripture Guide for Those Seeking Liberation (gCod gzhung thar dod ded dpon gyi dgongs pa rab tu gsal ba'i gyan)*, by Yongdzin Yeshe Gyaltsen.

An exhaustive list of masters whose works on Chöd are studied by present-day Gelugpa practitioners of Chöd is as follows: Buddha Shakyamuni, Arya Manjushri, Machig Labdrön, Aryadeva, Gyalwa Döndrub, Panchen Lungrig Gyatso, Dulzin Lodro Bepa

Dagpa Palden, Gyalwa Gendun Gyatso, Gyalwa Ensapa Losang Döndrub, Khedrub Sangye Yeshe, Panchen Losang Chökyi Gyaltsen, Dorje Zinpa Könchog Gyaltsen, Kyishong Ngawang Tenzin Trinle, Changya Ngawang Chöden, Kunkyen Jamyang Shepa Ngawang Tsöndru, Drubwang Losang Namgyal, Kachen Yeshe Gyaltsen, Dagpu Garwang Losang Chökyi Wangchug, Tuken Losang Chökyi Nyima, Yongzin Drongtsewa Losang Tsultim, Yongzin Guge-wa, Ngul-chu Dharmabadra, Yangchen Drub-phe Dorje, Dagpo Kelsang Tenzin Kyedrub, Kyabje Phabongka Dechen Nyingpo, Geshe Lobsang Dönden, Kyabje Zong Rinpoche Losang Tsöndru, His Holiness 9th Khalka Jetsun Dampa.

39 Phabongka Rinpoche Dechen Nyingpo (1878-1941).

40 See note 6 above.

41 Machig's *Great Explanation*, known in Tibetan as *Namshe Chenmo (Phung po gzan skyur gyi rnam bshad gcod kyi don gsal byed)*. This text has been translated by Sarah Harding as *Machig's Complete Explanation: Clarifying the Meaning of Chöd, A Complete Explanation of Casting Out the Body as Food* (Ithaca, N.Y.: Snow Lion Publications, 2003).

42 This son was Gyalwa Dondrub. In a prayer request to his mother in the Shiwa Lamzab Chöd tradition he sings,

> Mother, first you gave me birth,
> Then provided all material needs.
> Finally you showed me the birthless sphere.
> Lord Mother Labdrön, I beseech!

43 *Lama Chöpa (Bla ma mchod pa)* by Panchen Losang Chökyi Gyaltsen. A recording of the English translation in verse, chanted to traditional melodies by David Molk together with members of Tibet Center, New York, is available from Ganden Samten Ling, Morning Glory Ranch, Big Sur, California 93920.

The sadhana, or meditative system and manual, commented upon here is *Dedicating the Illusory Body as Ganachakra, Promoting the Experience of Means and Wisdom, Wealth of the Ganden Practice Lineage (sGyu lus tshog su sngo ba)*, included as Appendix I of the present volume. The traditional melodies are recorded on the CD available from Snow Lion Publications. This text has also been translated as *Chöd: Cutting Off the Truly-Existent "I"* by Lama Thubten Zopa Rinpoche (Boston: Wisdom Publications, 1983).

44 *Dedicating the Illusory Body as Ganachakra, Promoting the Experience of Means and Wisdom, Wealth of the Ganden Practice Lineage (sGyu lus tshog su sngo ba)*, included as Appendix I of the present volume.

45 Tsa-tsa statues: small plaster cast images of gurus or deities.

46 Ultimate bodhichitta must be based in conventional bodhichitta. If wisdom realizing emptiness is divorced from conventional bodhichitta, it is not ultimate bodhichitta.

47 *Lamrim*: stages of the path teachings. A prayer for blessings to experience the stages of the path can be found in Appendix II, in the section beginning "Bless me to correctly rely on the Guru."

48 *Seven Days in Fearsome Sites (gNyan khrod zhag bdun ma)*. This empowerment is given over the course of seven days during which the disciple receives daily empowerments, transmissions, and instructions related to Chöd. Each night, the disciple is sent out by the guru to practice all night in a different power site. It authorizes practice of the "Hundred Springs Retreat" *(chu mig brgya tsa)*, which is a wandering retreat done on the basis of the yidam Tröma Nagmo (Khros ma nag mo) and the Chöd practice known in Tibetan as *Shiwa Lam Zab (Zhi ba lam zab)*, *Profound Path of Peace*. The lineage of this practice,

referred to in the tradition as the "Dakini Lineage," comes from Machig Labdrön to Gyälwa Dondrub, Khambuyale (Machig's grandson, who received it from her directly), Tönyön Latön, Kugom Chöseng, and so on in one lineage, as well as through another profound ear-whispered lineage up to the Gelugpa's E Lama Geleg Pelzang, Losang Yeshe, Gendün Gyaltsen, Geleg Rabgye, and Lhatsül Rinpoche, up to Kundeling Rinpoche, Khalka Jetsün Dampa Rinpoche, and others of the elder present generation. The Tibetan text for this practice has been translated as *Profound Path of Machig's Ear Whispered Lineage, A Convenient Daily Practice* by David Molk (privately printed, 1996).

49 More time is spent at the first, midpoint, and last sites; the practitioner moves a "stone's throw" between sites.

50 For the hundred springs retreat, it is not necessary that there be an actual spring at every site. The sites are visualized as charnel grounds, whether they are in fact or not, and among the characteristics of each charnel ground is a body of water.

51 Three overwhelmings: Tib. *zil gnon gsum.*

52 This is how to perform the first "overwhelming," the overwhelming of place. The second and third overwhelmings, not explicitly mentioned here, are overwhelming of gods and ghosts and overwhelming of self. Overwhelming of gods and ghosts is done, from the heart of oneself as the Deity, by emanating light and wrathful deities that gather all the gods and ghosts, even timid or reluctant ones, to come around one and prevent them from leaving. Overwhelming of self is done by visualizing one's mind going out with one's breath to mix with space, and meditating on emptiness. The sadhana has been supplemented with recitations from the oral tradition (in parentheses, pp. 000) connected with these latter two overwhelmings.

53 Machig Labdrön encircled by white Vajradakini in the east, yellow Ratnadakini in the south, red Padmadakini in the west, and green Karmadakini in the north.

54 In this four-armed aspect, the first right hand holds a vajra; the first left hand, a Prajnaparamita Sutra. The second two hands are in the mudra of meditative equipoise.

55 With the four dakinis surrounding Machig Labdrön in the center, the other yidams mentioned are situated as follows:

	Chakrasamvara	
Guhyasamaja	Machig Labdrön	Yamantaka
	Hevajra	

56 Actual bodhichitta is attained when it becomes spontaneous and unfabricated. Aspiring bodhichitta is the aspiration to attain enlightenment for the sake of all sentient beings. It can be maintained ritually, and is protected in this and future lives by keeping certain precepts. Engaging bodhichitta is engaging in the six perfections with the aspiration to attain enlightenment for the sake of all sentient beings and is generated by taking the eighteen root and forty-six secondary Bodhisattva vows. Bodhisattva vows, once received from the guru, are renewed daily through practices such as Six-Session Guru Yoga.

57 In the sadhana, the aspect is Vajravarahi.

58 The five syllables are OM, AH, HUM, SVA, and HA.

59 The outer form of Vajravarahi has two faces in Padampa Sangye's lineage. The first face, the "conventional" face, is that of Vajravarahi in her usual aspect. The second face, the "ultimate" face, is that of a three-eyed boar emerging from the right side of her head, looking up to the right.

60 All mother beings: sentient beings who have all been one's mother, as explained below.

61 For the prayer to the Mahamudra lineage gurus; see Appendix II, pp. 000.

62 From *Annihilation of Self-grasping (bDag 'dzin tshar gcod)*; this text is also excerpted for the Chöd Ganachakra in Appendix II, pp. 000.

63 The yogic conduct (*spyod pa*) of an ascetic: here, the Tantric behavior of going wandering as a yogi, working miracles for the benefit of beings, as a means to completing the accumulations necessary for full enlightenment.

64 "Released" (*grol*) refers to the "liberation of the consciousness" of a harmful spirit in the context of wrathful Tantric action.

65 The *Thirty-four Deeds* (Tib. *sKyes rabs so bzhi pa*) is the Tibetan anthology of Jataka tales, or stories of the previous lives of the Buddha, translated from Ashvaghosha's *Jatakamala.* The thirty-four deeds include ten deeds of generosity, ten of ethics, ten of patience, and four of diligence. This text is taught annually by the Ganden Tripa, the head of the Gelug Tradition, during the Great Prayer Festival at the beginning of the Tibetan new year.

66 The full account is published as *The Prince Who Became a Cuckoo, A Tale of Liberation*, by Lama Lodrö of Drepung, translated and edited by Lama Geshe Wangyal (New York: Theatre Arts Books, 1982).

67 The first way, the MA-DANG-LHA-YI-KA-DRO damaru rhythm is played three times; the second way, seven times.

68 The male-female union is considered to be implicit in the case of Highest Yoga Tantra yidam deities whose aspect is that of a solitary male or female deity.

69 These three Tantric systems are the three primary yidam practices in Gelug.

70 Sadaprarudita: Buddha tells his story in the *Eight Thousand Verse Perfection of Wisdom Sutra*

71 The three parts are (1) a torma for the direction protectors, referred to in the following paragraph of the commentary—Indra, Agni, Yama, rakshasas, Water God, Wind God, yakshas, Bhuta, Brahma, Sun God, Moon God, Rahula, gods of the seven planets, constellations, nagas, vidyadharas, and kings; (2) a torma for *dön* spirits (Tib. *gdon,* Skt. *graha*), interfering spirits who can be pacified and brought into service if propitiated; and (3) a torma for *geg* (Tib. *bgegs,* Skt. *bigna*), malevolent spirits and obstructive conditions.

72 Torma (*gtor ma*) refers to a ritual offering cake, in this case "handprint" tormas made by squeezing a roll of tea-moistened tsampa in the fist, leaving the print of the fingers and thumb on it. This particular mealtime torma offering is made in conjunction with recitation of the *Three Jewels Recollection Sutra.* Briefly described, after praising the qualities of Buddha, Dharma, and Sangha, the merit of offering the meal to the Buddhas is dedicated to rebirth in Sukhavati, enjoyment of Dharma and enjoyment of the food of samadhi. Then after further praises and dedications, the first portion of the meal is offered to the Guru. Then successive offerings are made to the buddhas and bodhisattvas, yidam deities, and dharma protectors. After partaking of the meal the handprint tormas are offered to Hariti, her 500 children, and harmful spirits and obstructers. Finally, homage and mantra of the Buddha Jeweled Fire Light is recited, followed by dedications on behalf of the patrons of the meal and all sentient beings.

73 Land of the Thirty-three: Indra's heaven.

74 Vaibhashika is the first of the four tenet systems, the other three being Sautrantika, Chittamatra, and Madhyamaka.

75 The expression "view of the transitory collection" (Tib. *'jig tshogs la lta ba*) refers to grasping oneself to be inherently existent rather than grasping other people or phenomena to be inherently existent.

76 Actual absorption of concentration (*bsam gtan gyi dngo gzhi'i snyoms 'jug*) and preparatory

or approach stage of concentration (*bsam gtan gyi nyer bsdogs*). If actual absorption of concentration is attained, one's mind attains a state similar to that of a deva of the form realm. The actual concentrations are equivalent to the states of the form and formless realms. Whereas in non-Buddhist paths attainment of actual form and formless realm concentrations may be considered indispensable to liberation, in a Buddhist path, a mind that is still of the desire realm, that of the approach to the level of the first concentration, is considered to be a sufficient level of concentrative absorption to serve as a basis for the supramundane path's penetrative insight realizing selflessness and the attainment of liberation and superior paths.

77 "Hidden object" derives from the threefold categorization of phenomena into (1) manifest phenomena, initially accessible to direct perception; (2) hidden phenomena that, while accessible to direct perception, can be initially realized only through logical inference; and (3) extremely hidden phenomena that are accessible to direct perception by omniscient mind, which can be realized initially only through scriptural inference.

78 Suppleness is one of the eleven virtuous mental factors, which functions to overcome all disfunctionality of body and mind, making the body and mind perfectly usable for application to virtue. It is only once this has been experienced that the object of a fully qualified shamata, or calm abiding, meditation is attained.

79 Seventy Topics (Tib. *don bdun cu*), a summary of the subjects studied in connection with the *Ornament of Realizations* (Skt. *Abhisamayalamkara*), Maitreya's commentary on the hidden meaning of the Perfection of Wisdom sutras. The Seventy Topics are studied as a preliminary to beginning the first major course in a Geshe's education.

80 In Tibetan, "permanence" is *tag pa* and "impermanence" is *mi tag pa*, a negation or exclusion of *tag pa*. Thus, as in English, the term for impermanence is a negation of its opposite. In a common set of definitions for the pair, however, the opposite is the case. Impermanence is defined as momentary, *skad cig ma*, while permanence is defined as its negation—not being momentary, *skad cig ma ma yin pa*.

81 Only something that is the same in name and meaning is considered to be "one." Synonyms are considered different because, although they have the same meaning, their names are different.

82 *Ganden Lhagyema*, "Hundred Deities of the Joyous Land," is the major short guru yoga of Je Tsongkhapa from the Segyu lineage of Gelugpa.

83 Collected Topics (Tib. *bsdus grwa*) and Mind and Cognition (Tib. *blo rigs*).

84 *The Flower Ornament Sutra* (Skt. *Avatamsaka;* Tib. *mDo phal bo che*). English translation: *The Flower Ornament Scripture*, by Thomas Cleary (Boston: Shambhala Publications, 1993). The lines cited here can be found on pp. 312-319 of the one-volume edition. This scripture mainly focuses on the bodhisattva's austerities and code of ethics. When Je Tsongkhapa was in retreat at Olga Chölung undergoing purification, he read this sutra and it helped reinforce his practice.

85 In Tibetan, the four maras are *phung po'i bdud, nyon mongs pa'i bdud, lha'i bu yi bdud,* and *'chi bdag gi bdud.*

86 Four Hundred Practices: Tib. *brgya bzhi.*

87 This is an empowerment of Buddha Shakyamuni in the aspect of a subduer of Mara; Tib. *Thub dbang bdud btul ma.*

88 Obstructive, nonobstructive, joyfulness and arrogance maras: Tib. *thogs bcas, thogs med, dga' brod,* and *snyems byed.*

89 Spiritual grounds refers to the arya bodhisattva stages, beginning from the path of seeing.

90 "Disturbances": Tib. *lhong.*

91 Tibetan *lama* (*bla ma*) and Sanskrit *guru* are here taken as synonymous and used interchangeably.

92 Awareness of the non-inherent existence of the three spheres of dedication refers to awareness of the non-inherent existence of the dedicator, the act of dedicating, and the object of dedication.

93 Beings with and without breath: sentient beings breathlessly tormented in samsara, as well as those taking a "breather," those who have fallen to an extreme of solitary peace.

94 *The Precious Garland of Activities of the Chöd Feast Gathering* (*Tshogs las rin chen phreng ba*), by Karmapa Rangjung Dorje. English translation by David Molk (privately printed, 1998).

95 This holds for the Ganden Chöd sadhana presented in Appendix I, which the commentary follows. In the Profound Path of Peace (Shiwa Lamzab) Dakini lineage used for the Hundred Springs Retreat, the damaru is played in the reverse direction.

96 The damaru is first played with the following patterns (in standard 4/4 time, short beats equal eighth notes and long beats equal quarter notes, with slight variations in tempo) and mnemonic devices in succession before beginning the ritual chant:

DRUM-DRUM, rhythm in beats of short, short (9x), twice, while reciting the GATE mantra twice;

MA-DANG-LHA-YI-KA-DRO, twice, the rhythm in beats of short, short, long, long, short, short (2x);

CHOM-DEN-DE, twice, with rhythm in beats of short, short, long; short, short, long;

MA-DANG-KA-DRO, twice, the rhythm in beats of short, short, short, short (2x);

MA-DANG, twice, with rhythm in beats of short, short (2x).

At this point chanting of the sadhana begins. The MA-DANG-LHA-YI-KA-DRO is the main damaru rhythm used throughout.

97 *sGyu lus tshogs su sngo ba thabs shes nyams kyi pogs 'don dga' ldan sgrub rgyud spyi nor.* Kyabje Phabongka Dechen Nyingpo's dates are 1878-1941.

98 *Chöd Instruction Guide for Those Seeking Liberation,* known as *Thardö Depön (gCod kyi gdams pa thar 'dod kyi ded dpon)* by Panchen Losang Chökyi Gyaltsen, is translated in "A Study of the Profound Path of gCod: The Mahayana Buddhist Meditation Tradition of Tibet's Great Woman Saint Machig Labdron," by Carol Diane Savvas (PhD diss., University of Wisconsin, Madison, 1990), pp. 400-427.

99 *Ornament to the Ganden Practice Lineage Teachings: Ganden Drubgyu Tenpay Tzegyen (dGa' ldan sgrub rgyud bstan pa'i mdzes rgyan).*

100 Sugatas' Children: children of the buddhas, i.e., bodhisattvas, those who will "grow up" to become Buddhas.

101 These verses of supplication to the lineage gurus following the verse to Je Tsongkhapa Losang Dragpa up to this point, as well as the three verses of auspiciousness at the end, were actually composed by Mochog Rinpoche. The following two verses were added by disciples of Kyabje Zong Rinpoche. Since Kyabje Zong Rinpoche received Chöd transmissions from Kyabje Pabongka's disciple, the great Yeshe Jampa Rinpoche, as well as Kyabje Pabongka, a verse of supplication to Yeshe Jampa Rinpoche precedes the verse to Kyabje Zong Rinpoche in which he is referred to by his name Losang Tsöndru.

102 Avadhuti: the central psychic channel.

103 This Chöd mind training prayer is by the first Jamyang Zhepa Ngawang Tsöndru.

104 *Zab lam gcod kyi rnal 'byor dang 'drel ba'i tshogs mchod 'bul tshul su bkod pa.* Also included in Carol Diane Savvas, op. cit., pp. 439-472. Compiled from *Guru Puja, Dedicating the Illu-*

sory Body as Ganachakra, Heruka Vajrayogini Tantra, Annihilation of Self-Grasping, and other sources. Translations by David Molk.

105 Kukkutapada: a mountain in Magadha.

106 Second Buddha: *kun mkhyen gnyis pa,* literally, a second omniscient one.

107 As recorded on the CD, the oral tradition may abbreviate here, by going directly to the next section, the requests to the close lineage gurus

108 Gwalwa Losang Döndrub: Gyälwa Ensapa.

109 Full enlightenment is referred to as the accomplishment of one's own and others' purposes.

110 It is at this point that the CD recording continues.

111 The additional two are added when the meditation is done in its Tantric context. The third point is that the experience is great bliss, and the fourth is that, upon the basis of the first three, one imputes the divine pride of being the deity.

A DVD recording is available of Kyabje Zong Rinpoche's instruction on the chanting of Chöd, in Tibetan with English subtitles. This is not a complete Chöd but a session of instruction to Western students in which Kyabje Zong Rinpoche taught the Tibetan chanting of each of the different melodies by repeating verses excerpted from the Chöd practices that are translated in appendices I and II of this book. For more information, contact:

Zong Labrang
Gaden Monastic University
P.O. Tibetan Colony - 581411
Mundgod, Distt North Kanara
Karnataka State
INDIA

email: zonglibrary@yahoo.co.in